Jesus on Gardening

David Muskett

Onwards and Upwards Publishers

3 Radfords Turf
Cranbrook
Exeter
EX5 7DX
United Kingdom

www.onwardsandupwards.org

Copyright © David Muskett 2016

The right of David Muskett to be identified as the author of this work has been asserted by the author in accordance with the Copyright, Designs and Patents Act 1988.

Printed in the UK.

ISBN:	978-1-911086-28-4
Typeface:	Sabon LT
Graphic design:	LM Graphic Design

About the Author

David is married with two grown up daughters, and lives and gardens in Surrey where he is Methodist Minister in the East Solent and Downs Circuit. Ordained in the Church of England in 1990, David has served churches in Bedfordshire and Surrey, moving to his present appointment in 2010 and transferring to the Methodist Church in 2013.

To contact the author, please write to:
davidjmuskett@gmail.com

Endorsements

This charming and illuminating little book will engage the general reader, deepen the faith of new Christians and serve as an exemplar for the preacher on how to be down-to-earth, true to Scripture and gently inspirational when crafting and delivering sermons. Warmly recommended!

Revd David Sutcliffe
Pastor, Hearsall Baptist Church, Coventry

I have to be honest and say that a book on gardening is not the first one I pick up when I wander around a bookshop – unlike David, I am not a gardener! However, a book with Jesus in the title would make me pick it up as the nurture of my own faith is a passion of my life! David, sharing with us his own faith, and with great skill, develops the Gospel accounts of Jesus and those times when horticulture and agriculture feature in his earthly life and ministry. David is an accomplished preacher and this is seen in the way the sermons are written and developed so that we have a better understanding of the call of Christ in our own lives and as we face the challenge of discipleship and faith today. I would encourage preachers to use this resource to cultivate their own preaching, and pray that all will find, through this book, their own relationship with God and Jesus more firmly rooted.

The Rev'd Andrew de Ville
Superintendent Minister, The Methodist Church.

'Jesus on Gardening' by David Muskett is a clever and creative book, linking together many of Jesus' teachings drawn from the rural life He saw around Him. Written in an easy-to-read, conversational style David manages to bring to life the agricultural practices of two millennia ago and apply them to us today with the sort of punch that Jesus' first hearers must have felt. Each chapter begins with the relevant Bible passage which is helpful as it means the book can be read anywhere without having to have a chunky Bible to hand. It also ensures that the 'sermons' remain biblically focussed – always a good idea for preachers! I would warmly recommend this book not only for budding and experienced preachers but for anyone who wants to 'ring the changes' and bring a fresh approach to their daily Quiet Times or devotions. Most chapters refer to other Bible passages beyond the main text (usually printed out) and so could provide reflective material for several days.

Keith Field
Cranleigh Baptist Church

These sermons are easy to read – but not easy reading. I like the clear, simple language. The good humour of the preacher shines through his words, as does his careful observation of everyday life on the farm and in the garden. He's learned that from Jesus' way of teaching. And with the sayings of Jesus he leads us beneath the everyday surface, to the root of things, to dig up a selection of challenges for everyday Christians. These are pastoral sermons in more senses than one. They are an enjoyable walk through field and garden, but they nourish our faith too. David tills the soil well.

Paul Johns
Methodist preacher; former Director of the College of Preachers

Having just acquired a new garden I was delighted to receive this book. David emphasises that Jesus' teachings are not a treatise on gardening, but an everyday way of understanding more about the Kingdom of God and life within that Kingdom. With gentle humour and theological insight David takes the reader through the agricultural aspects of Jesus' teaching. Ideal for personal devotion as well as for sermon material, this book has enabled my 'garden pottering' to be an opportunity for reflection on God's word.

The final section of the book on sermon preparation, preaching and listening provides very helpful guidelines for both the new and the more experienced preacher. Those who are not preachers will find this section gives suggestions for personal reflection on passages of Scripture and on sermons! I warmly recommend this book – an easy read with spiritual depth that will help you grow in your faith.

Jeanette Richardson

Contents

Jesus on Gardening

Foreword by Andrew Wood

It is often said that many Christians today are poor stewards of creation. Sometimes we barely comprehend the impact of our actions on the natural world. In this collection of sermons, David Muskett helps us in two important ways. He reminds us that Jesus lived close to the world of crops, plants and trees and drew inspiration to talk about the Kingdom of God from this understanding. And he makes a connection between the world of the New Testament and that of contemporary people, between the teaching of Jesus and our hearing of it today.

Jesus the Gardener is a startling and perhaps strange image, and yet it is in gardens that so many people encounter the beauty of nature and the work to create something from the soil, or soils as one of the parables has it. In Jesus' care and understanding of the world around us, and in nature's own startling life, death and rebirths we find echoes of the Kingdom. David mines this rich vein of imagery, story and parable to help us understand eternal truths about life, death, resurrection and discipleship. In doing this he shows us Jesus' teaching on the kingdom in a new light. Whether it is reflections on growth, the workforce, or the gardens of Easter, this book is insightful and direct in its retelling and its preaching of the good news. David is both a gardener and a preacher and both are in evidence here, for the benefit of the whole church. In engaging with the text, and living in the Bible story, he poses that great question of the preacher: "Where does this leave us today?"

Andrew Wood
Chair of Southampton Methodist District

Jesus on Gardening

Introduction

This book was conceived while I served as Vicar of Milford in Surrey and developed while Associate Minister at Emmanuel Church Stoughton, Guildford, but written while Methodist Minister at Haslemere in Surrey. It has taken some time! I am grateful to the congregations at Emmanuel and in the East Solent and Downs Methodist Circuit for their patience with my phrases and questions that feature in this book.

I found myself preaching at 8am services or midweek communions on several of the parables and sayings of Jesus that relate to 'gardening' in its broadest sense encompassing horticulture and agriculture. I occasionally referred to this as 'Jesus on Gardening', particularly when preaching on the Parable of the Sower on a Wednesday morning at Emmanuel. The phrase stuck and I decided to collect together some sermons on those parables and sayings. When putting the list together it also seemed appropriate to include some other garden-related events. The last few sermons therefore have a slightly different feel to them as they are on events from Maundy Thursday night through to Easter Day.

While writing, I read David Bracewell's excellent collection of sermons entitled '15 Minutes to Wake the Dead'. In it he includes some short sections on the practicalities of preaching. I am indebted to him for the idea of the 'Sermon Notes for Preachers and Listeners'. These are not the same as David's sections but have arisen from my own tutoring of preachers with the College of Preachers. They centre round questions worth asking and a desire for both preachers and listeners to get the most out of sermons. I hope they prompt thought about the process of preaching for both preachers and listeners alike.

Most discussions of preaching include something about length. Some congregations start fidgeting if a sermon is more than ten minutes; others feel cheated if it is less than twenty-five. These would mostly take about fifteen minutes to preach as they are. They are therefore slightly shorter than many I preach now in a Methodist setting and slightly longer than many Anglican 8am congregations I have known. That shouldn't make a difference to their use. Preachers will be used to the 'adopt and adapt' principle with sermon ideas. I hope that those who more often listen than speak during the sermon will find that these give food for thought and supplement their weekly diet.

David Muskett
Haslemere

1

Jesus on Soil

The Parable of the Sower

Matthew 13:1-9,18-23; Mark 4:1-20; Luke 8:1-15

That same day Jesus went out of the house and sat by the lake. Such large crowds gathered round him that he got into a boat and sat in it, while all the people stood on the shore. Then he told them many things in parables, saying: "A farmer went out to sow his seed. As he was scattering the seed, some fell along the path, and the birds came and ate it up. Some fell on rocky places, where it did not have much soil. It sprang up quickly, because the soil was shallow. But when the sun came up, the plants were scorched, and they withered because they had no root. Other seed fell among thorns, which grew up and choked the plants. Still other seed fell on good soil, where it produced a crop – a hundred, sixty or thirty times what was sown. Whoever has ears, let them hear."

...

"Listen then to what the parable of the sower means: when anyone hears the message about the kingdom and does not understand it, the evil one comes and snatches away what was sown in their heart. This is the seed sown along the path. The

seed falling on rocky ground refers to someone who hears the word and at once receives it with joy. But since they have no root, they last only a short time. When trouble or persecution comes because of the word, they quickly fall away. The seed falling among the thorns refers to someone who hears the word, but the worries of this life and the deceitfulness of wealth choke the word, making it unfruitful. But the seed falling on good soil refers to someone who hears the word and understands it. This is the one who produces a crop, yielding a hundred, sixty or thirty times what was sown."

Some years ago Alan Titchmarsh did a series on TV called 'How to be a Gardener'. He began, not with advice about tools or seed catalogues or how to choose good, healthy plants, but with soil. Similarly, this story, commonly called the Parable of the Sower, is more about soil that sowing.

In looking at Jesus' 'advice' to gardeners it seems right to start this way; it is very hard to garden successfully unless you have some idea what sort of soil you have. The central and often repeated thesis of this book is that although Jesus talked a lot about many aspects of horticulture, agriculture and even viticulture, he was not really giving advice on gardening except incidentally. When he talked about gardening it was always by way of illustration about something else. So I start with soil, like Alan Titchmarsh and like Jesus, because it is there that things grow; what grows and how well it grows is largely dependent on the kind of soil you have.

The Parable of the Sower can just as well be called the Parable of the Soil.

Jesus teaches vividly from scenes that would have been familiar to his hearers. In this context Jesus is by the shore but I imagine there were hills going up beside the lake on which there may have been a farmer walking up and down sowing seed.

Modern readers now picture a tractor moving across a hillside with a seed drill on the back and neatly ploughed furrows. It is worth remembering that farmers' fields in first century Palestine were not like that. The nearest tractor was twenty centuries away and ploughs were pulled by oxen. Fields would have contained stones, the largest of which might have been laboriously moved away and piled at the side by hand. The seed drill would also not be invented for 2000 years so the process of sowing was a very imprecise broadcasting or scattering. The farmer would have walked up and down with a basket of seed under one arm simply throwing the seed around.

The field that Jesus pictures has certain features to it. There's a path, perhaps along one side of the field, perhaps across the middle. This area would have been baked hard and flat meaning that the seed simply lay on the surface very obvious to birds looking for food. The first lesson about sowing seed is that the soil needs to be prepared – dug over and loosened so the seed can fall in and be covered over. The packed soil of a path leaves the seed vulnerable to being snatched away and never getting started.

Another feature of the field is a rocky place. This might be the area where large stones have been moved to the side. Or it might be a place where there are large stones just below the surface. Either way, there was hardly any soil for the young plant to put down roots. It got off to a good start but with no depth of soil it dried out quickly. The top layer of soil always dries out quickly but it is surprising how much moisture there can be lower down even in the hottest and driest of summers. Jesus points out that these plants on the rocky area cannot get enough moisture and so wither and die, being vulnerable to drought.

A third feature of this field is weeds. It has been said that a weed is a plant in the wrong place. I suspect this is a case of the right place but the wrong plant. Jesus teaches more about dealing with weeds in another story, so here we just have to accept that this is the way it was. We will hear his advice on weed killer in another chapter. It sounds as though this is a good part of the field and these plants have either grown from other seed blown by the wind or they are perennials that come back year after year. They are vigorous, fast growing bullies of the garden that flourish in these conditions. Some of the farmer's seed falls among them but can't get enough light or space or moisture amid the competition and doesn't come to anything.

We've now become quite familiar with this farmer's field and we're starting to wonder how anyone ever grew anything with the path and the rocks and the weeds. But Jesus assures us that the farmer has been able to clear some rocks and there are places where the weeds haven't got a hold and perhaps the path does only go round the edge. There is good soil – soil that has been broken up, that goes down deep and hasn't been dominated by other plants. In this soil the seeds broadcast by the farmer can fall in and put down roots, find moisture and put up shoots, and grow unhindered until they bear fruit.

Just to show that in this soil the results can be extraordinarily good, Jesus tells us that the grain in the ear may be thirty, sixty or a hundred times what was sown. That sounds like exaggeration for effect to me, what is sometimes called rabbinic hyperbole, but it gets the point across. It also serves to underline the point that Jesus is not talking about the effects that you can expect in your garden if you plant in good soil. Any gardener will tell you that the rate of return varies with different kinds of plants. The point is that, as usual, Jesus is not really talking about gardening.

So what is he talking about?

Well, on the face of it he explains the parable. The seed sown is the word of God and the different areas of the field are different ways in which it is received so the success or otherwise of the growth of the plant is about how well (or otherwise) God's word gets on. Jesus gives us warning that if the good news of his kingdom doesn't sink in, it will be snatched away. He tells us that if it is not fed and given depth, an initial enthusiasm for God's ways will wither and die. Jesus also warns that there are many distractions that can crowd out the growth of his word. The obvious encouragement is that there is good soil and the good news of the kingdom will grow and flourish and bear fruit in the right conditions.

I'm sure we can understand that and you're probably a step ahead of me now. You probably know where this is going because even that sounds too much like gardening and not enough like the challenging teaching we're used to from Jesus. The point where we stick the knife in and twist it is with the inevitable question, "Which sort of soil are you?"

If the seed of the word of God, in the form of the good news of his kingdom coming among us in Jesus, is sown in you, what happens to it? Where in this field would we find you?

Are you part of the path? Do you have a hard outer layer that means the seed can't get any roots down at all and just lays vulnerable to being snatched away by the first other idea that comes along?

Or are you in that rocky area where the soil is not very deep. Maybe you're quite enthusiastic about your faith growing from a recent visit to church, but you don't go regularly, or you don't read your bible or pray very often, or you don't really listen to sermons or attend a home group. If you are not taking opportunities to feed and water God's ways, it will be hard to see them grow strong in terms of words and actions that influence others or spread the values of God's kingdom in love, joy, peace, patience, kindness, goodness, faithfulness, gentleness, self-control...[1]

You might be in a good part of the field with all the right opportunities but you struggle to take them. Maybe you are a member of a home group for Bible study and prayer and the mutual encouragement that comes from meeting with and praying with and for others. Maybe you have a good church, with encouraging and challenging teaching. Maybe you have everything going for you but you like to play golf on Sunday mornings, or Wednesday evenings is also when the Horticultural Society meets or it just seems as though you always get invitations to something else just when you thought you might get along. The cares of other aspects of life come crowding in and suddenly there's no room for the nurture that God's word needs in your life if it is to come to fruition.

Or perhaps you bear fruit. Perhaps just a tiny seed of God's good news, planted almost unknowingly in your life by a comment of a friend or a chance reading of an article or a visit to church at Christmas, has been well looked after through regular attendance at church and being involved in a small group and you can see that your life has changed to reflect God's ways in the neighbourhoods and communities where you live and work.

You will know if you're bearing fruit because your life will take on more and more of the characteristics that St Paul describes as the fruit of the Spirit: love, joy, peace, patience, kindness, goodness, faithfulness, gentleness and self-control. And you'll see your life and your words having an effect for good on the lives of those you meet and speak with.

---

[1] Galatians 5:22-23

Jesus' challenge in his Parable of the Soil is to be good soil. Where the analogy breaks down, as all analogies do somewhere, is that the difference between us and soil is that the soil can have no influence over where it is in the field. We can decide to be good soil and nurture the word of God in us.

2

Jesus on Flowers

Flowers of the Field

Matthew 6:25-34; Luke 12:22-31

"Therefore I tell you, do not worry about your life, what you will eat or drink; or about your body, what you will wear. Is not life more than food, and the body more than clothes? Look at the birds of the air; they do not sow or reap or store away in barns, and yet your heavenly Father feeds them. Are you not much more valuable than they? Can any one of you by worrying add a single hour to your life?

"And why do you worry about clothes? See how the flowers of the field grow. They do not labour or spin. Yet I tell you that not even Solomon in all his splendour was dressed like one of these. If that is how God clothes the grass of the field, which is here today and tomorrow is thrown into the fire, will he not much more clothe you – you of little faith? So do not worry, saying, 'What shall we eat?' or 'What shall we drink?' or 'What shall we wear?' For the pagans run after all these things, and your heavenly Father knows that you need them. But seek first his kingdom and his righteousness, and all these things will be given to you as well. Therefore do not worry

*about tomorrow, for tomorrow will worry about itself. Each
day has enough trouble of its own."*

It is said that farmers are more anxious than people of any other
occupation. At present we might think they have good reason to be
with all the uncertainties about the price they might get for their
products. They have to decide what to grow before they know what
price they might eventually get for it. Unlike many markets, the
market for our food is driven by the 'middle man', the person who
buys the raw material from the grower and passes it on through
manufacture, processing and packaging to retail and consumers.

Supermarkets control the price they sell goods at and the price
they buy the raw materials. Farmers simply have to sell at whatever
price they can get – sometimes simply to cut their losses.

If price wasn't enough to worry about, you can add in factors
such as disease and the weather, either of which might destroy a
harvest or leave the farmers with nothing to sell even if they could get
a price for it. Wet summers, foot and mouth disease, dry springs, and
so on, have all given farmers plenty to worry about.

No doubt many of us have things to worry about. Many people
might be saying that their occupations give them plenty to worry
about. Times of recession, austerity and cuts mean that many people
are worried as to whether they will have a job beyond the short term.
Others are worried about illness, frailty and the adequacy of their
pension arrangements. Still more are worried about their children,
their children's education, their children's housing or their children's
children as well as their own mortgages and investments.

Farmers might traditionally be the most anxious people but many
people think they can give them a run for their money, and no one
seems exempt from worry.

And then we hear Jesus say, "Do not worry." In this short section
of the Sermon on the Mount Jesus says, "Do not worry," three times:

*"...do not worry about your life, what you will eat or drink;
or about your body, what you will wear." (NIV)*

*"...do not worry, saying, 'What shall we eat?' or 'What shall
we drink?' or 'What shall we wear?'" (NIV)*

"...do not worry about tomorrow." (NIV)

His first comparison, in order to demonstrate that there is no need to worry, is with the birds of the air. They don't sow or reap or store away in barns. In other words, they're not farmers. In human development terms, the birds of the air are nomadic hunter gatherers. They don't worry about how to live and yet God feeds them. So is Jesus undermining the whole gardening/farming idea?

Then Jesus compares those who worry about clothes with the lilies of the field. They don't labour or spin. In other words, they're not weavers or textile manufacturers and yet God clothes them. So perhaps Jesus is undermining the clothing industry?

Clearly there would be huge implications if Christians were to conclude from Jesus' remarks here that not worrying about these things meant we were not to engage in work in these areas. It seems to me that would be a ludicrous conclusion. So there must be something else to it.

Let's remember that worrying about something is not the same as being concerned about something.

Worry is an inward-looking, mental exercise that goes around in circles simply chewing over something difficult or problematic.

Concern about something is more positive and involves working out what to do about it. To be concerned with something is to engage with it, working towards the solution to the problem or how to overcome the difficulty.

Jesus says we should not worry, but that does not let us off the hook of being concerned about our food and drink and clothes. The birds don't worry, they don't sow or reap or store away in barns, but they do have to go out and look for food and find the seeds, berries and worms and eat them or take them back to their young in the nest. There is work to be done if you want to eat even if you are a bird.

Similarly with people, we cannot expect that not worrying means that everything will be given us on a plate without any effort on our part.

When it comes to grass and lilies, Jesus does comment on their beauty and, if we want a gardening comment from him, he seems in favour of cutting the grass. But once again Jesus is not really talking about gardening or farming. Lilies are beautiful, but it is not through their own efforts. Lilies, Jesus asserts, are turned out better than even King Solomon in all his finery.

It is no accident that these comments come in the Sermon on the Mount in the chapter where Jesus has taken a detailed excursus into the subject of prayer. In his model for prayer, known as the Lord's Prayer, Jesus has taught his followers to call God *"Father"* and here he refers to God as our *"heavenly Father"*.

There are two important connections to notice. Firstly, and most obviously in this section, God cares for us as his children, knows what we need and is longing to provide for us. Just as we would not see our children go in want, so God will not see us go without the basic necessities of life.

Clearly there are questions that can be raised about this in relation to those who starve and those who have no shelter. These questions are also complicated by the extent to which human action is responsible for people starving or being homeless.

The second connection to be made is on this question of worry. It seems that Jesus tells us not to worry in the same context as he teaches us to pray. The difference seems to be that worry is inward-looking, circular and unproductive whereas prayer is directed towards God. That's why we start our prayers by addressing him. Jesus taught us to pray, *"Our Father..."* Sometimes we might start with "Almighty God" or "Merciful Lord" or another form of address appropriate to the attributes of God which we think relevant to the subject, people and places on our minds.

Our worries stay with us but our concerns move towards solutions and our prayers are directed towards God, who can help us with our solutions. He may empower us; he may inspire others; he may show us that it is not a matter of such urgency as we thought.

That last point is made by Jesus' third "do not worry" in this passage: *"...do not worry about tomorrow, for tomorrow will worry about itself. Each day has enough trouble of its own."*

That is not to say that we shouldn't work today for tomorrow's food. It is not to say that we don't need to plan ahead. But it does say that worrying about tomorrow will not change tomorrow. There is enough trouble and concern, there are sufficient issues and problems and difficulties today, without worrying about what we may think of tomorrow.

It is all put in perspective by the phrase I haven't mentioned yet. It is the key to this section as it is the key to Jesus' teaching on prayer. *"But seek first his kingdom and his righteousness."*

He echoes what he has just taught about prayer: *"Our Father ... your kingdom come ... on earth as in heaven."*

It is practical and spiritual, worldly and heavenly. Seeking God's kingdom is to look for and work for the ways of God in the world. The ways of God – what happens when he rules – are the ways of peace, justice, love and mercy, and grace and care for others and our environment. Seeking God's righteousness is to look for and work for relationships and ways of behaving that are in accord with the ways of God, which value others and seek their peace and well-being, and act in ways that honour God and his creation.

Jesus draws from the natural order of birds and flowers and their lack of worry a lesson for us: seeking to follow the ways and works of God and directing our concerns to him at the right time will honour him and express the trust that he asks of us as our heavenly Father.

Paul summarised the approach when he wrote to the Philippians, *"Do not be anxious about anything, but in every situation, by prayer and petition, with thanksgiving, present your requests to God."*[2]

And in this passage Jesus simply gives us an explanation and illustration of the first part of the Lord's Prayer:

> *"Our Father in heaven, hallowed be your name, your kingdom come, your will be done, on earth as it is in heaven. Give us today our daily bread." (NIV)*
>
> ...
>
> *"Seek first his kingdom and his righteousness, and all these things will be given to you as well. Therefore do not worry about tomorrow, for tomorrow will worry about itself. Each day has enough trouble of its own." (NIV)*

---

[2] Philippians 4:6

3

Jesus on the Workforce (i)

Shortage of Labour at Harvest Time

Matthew 9:37-38

Then he said to his disciples, "The harvest is plentiful but the workers are few. Ask the Lord of the harvest, therefore, to send out workers into his harvest field." (NIV)

In many parts of this country you can walk and drive through the countryside in late July and early August and see fields ripe for a plentiful harvest. In places the fields stretch for acres and acres, mile upon mile. It is also true that in this country, even at harvest time, the workers are few. The reason for that these days is because not many are needed.

Since the agricultural and industrial revolutions of the 18th and 19th centuries and the ever increasing mechanisation of the 20th century fewer workers have been needed for formerly labour intensive jobs and the vast majority of our population has moved to towns and cities.

In Jesus' context historically, geographically and sociologically harvest was an activity that required much labour. Relatively speaking, there would have been vastly more workers in the fields. But it is relative. Jesus comments that the workers are few. Not few relative to the numbers that there would be in two thousand years' time, but few relative to the numbers required for the task.

As any gardener and any farmer will tell you, the harvest doesn't wait. When the crop is ripe, the crop is ripe, whether it is grain or marrows, and needs to be brought in to use for food or to store. There is a very narrow window for harvest. That's one of the reasons farmers tend to look worried and spend more time looking up at the sky than other members of the community. The weather needs to be right at the same time as the crops.

As Jesus looks around he sees that the harvest is ready and it's a good one. It looks as though the barns and the grain silos will be full. But he also notices that the workers are few. It is going to be a hard job to get the harvest in with this labour force in the time available.

And Jesus has the answer. It is basic commercial management practice really. If you don't have sufficient workforce for the job in hand, you need to take on more staff. The Royal Mail do it every year at Christmas. You could paraphrase Jesus for mail delivery: "The post is plentiful but the deliverers are few. Ask the Postmaster General therefore to send more postmen on to the streets." Or more generally, "Ask the one in charge to send the workers out to get on with it." That doesn't really require an agricultural college or management college or theological college training to work out. It gives us a small sociological insight into agricultural employment. Many agricultural workers today are hired on a more or less casual basis for seasonal work. It was almost entirely casual work in Jesus' time with workers hired by the day. So, there's a lot of harvest to get in – send a lot of workers to do it. Simple.

But why does Jesus concern himself with advice to local farmers? He is more than likely most qualified in working with wood and he has friends in the fishing business as well as a few ex-tax collectors and freedom fighters. Jesus knows enough about employment in local industries where his contemporaries and hearers would work to be able to make parallels.

As always we have to make the translation from the subject of Jesus' words to the subject he most usually spoke about. Typically, when Jesus spoke he had something to say about the kingdom of God and the way it worked, how God ruled it, how people in it behaved or how people find their place in it. So what's he talking about here if it's not about how many people you need to gather in the harvest?

Well, this comment comes at the end of Matthew 9. In this chapter Matthew has recorded the healing of the paralysed man who was lowered through the roof; he has called Matthew from his tax collecting booth and attended a party at Matthew's house; he's answered questions about fasting, healed a sick woman and raised Jairus' daughter from the dead. He's also healed two blind men and one who was demon possessed and unable to talk. This gave rise to controversy about how he was able to cast out demons.

That all adds up to a busy schedule with many people seeking help with various diseases and ailments. But in between there has been time for controversy, for answering questions and for preaching. Matthew's summary of the activity in the preceding verses says:

Jesus went through all the towns and villages, teaching in their synagogues, proclaiming the good news of the kingdom and healing every disease and sickness. [3]

But Jesus has also noticed something. He's noticed a hunger for what he has to offer: a hunger for healing and help; a hunger to hear what he has to say; but also a desire to understand who he is and what he's about on the part of ordinary people. He's also been confronted by those who distrust him or who feel threatened. The religious authorities have challenged him about casting out demons and about forgiveness of sins. Jesus insists that he has come to call sinners, that people are healed by faith, that he brings something new, requiring new wineskins.

What Jesus has noticed is that the people are ready for him, ready for his news, ready for the kingdom, ready to receive the new wine, the forgiveness and healing that come with being a part of the kingdom of God that he proclaims. The people are ready but their leaders, those who should be showing them the way to take hold of it, are unable to see what is in front of their noses. In other words, as Matthew puts it, *"they were harassed and helpless, like sheep without a shepherd."* [4]

---

[3] Matthew 9:35
[4] Matthew 9:36

Consequently, Jesus has compassion on them. He realizes the harvest of the kingdom is ripe; it is time to bring it in, time to grease up the combine and get out the grain trailers. He has also noticed that this could be a bumper harvest; the people ready to be brought into the kingdom barns are so many that the current workforce is going to be stretched. So he says to his disciples:

> "Ask the Lord of the harvest ... to send out workers into his harvest field."[5]

It's fairly clear, but I think we need to get it out in the open as to who's who in this parable. The Lord of the harvest is Jesus. So who are the workers likely to be who are sent into the harvest field? Equally clearly that's most likely to be the disciples. In other words, the disciples are to ask Jesus to send them to go and bring people into the kingdom.

That's got us to a reasonably satisfactory explanation of these verses but I think you might be sensing that it needs to come up to date a bit more. "Where does that leave us?" might be what you're asking. As so often with Jesus it comes back to us as a challenge.

Look around you. Look around you in your neighbourhood, in your workplace, in the places where you spend time – the leisure centre, the supermarket checkout, the pubs and coffee shops around town... Where do you see people who are ready; where do you see people who are harassed and helpless like sheep without a shepherd because their leaders don't lead or guide them in right pathways; where do you see people who are searching for meaning and eager to catch hold of anything that speaks of hope and purpose and a connection with something bigger and outside of themselves that can give value and meaning to life?

If you can see something of that around then the fields are ripe, the harvest is plentiful, and it is time to grease up the combine and get out the grain trailers – and take on the workforce to do the job. So Jesus says the same to us: *"Ask the Lord of the harvest, therefore, to send out workers into his harvest field."*

And like those disciples he spoke to originally, the workforce they ask him to send is formed by those who ask. In other words, ask him to send you into today's harvest field to bring in people that you meet

---

[5] Matthew 9:38 (NIV)

who are ripe, ready and eager for the kingdom and its values of wholeness, forgiveness and grace.

4

Jesus on Fruit Trees (i)

How Trees Are Recognised

Luke 6:43-45

[Jesus said,] "No good tree bears bad fruit, nor does a bad tree bear good fruit. Each tree is recognised by its own fruit. People do not pick figs from thorn-bushes, or grapes from briers. Good people bring good things out of the good stored up in their heart, and evil people bring evil things out of the evil stored up in their heart. For out of the overflow of the heart the mouth speaks."

Let's start with a quick horticultural quiz – no conferring.[6]

1. Q: What sort of fruit do you get from an apple tree?
    A: Apples – it's not meant to be difficult!

2. Q: What do you get from a plum tree?
    A: Plums. It doesn't get much easier!

---

[6] A rapport with the congregation is necessary here to get answers from them. But this sort of quiz usually prompts ready responses when they realise it is not a trick question (until you get to number 4 and then you have a bit of a laugh about it).

3. Q: How about a vine?
   A: That is a tiny bit more difficult because the answer isn't in the question. We get grapes from vines.

4. Q: What about a little nut tree?
   A: A silver nutmeg and a golden pear is the correct answer according to the nursery rhyme.

Jesus seems to agree. Not about little nut trees in particular but about fruit trees in general. In this horticultural tutorial he points out that you don't get figs off thorn bushes. We know what sort of tree you do get figs from, don't we?[7]

Jesus doesn't tell us what sort of fruit you get from thorn bushes but it could be blackberries. At least it would be in this country but Jesus wasn't in this country so he may simply have been referring to the kind of thorn bushes that were used to make the crown of thorns. I was going to say these were rather pointless bushes but of course points are exactly what they did have. Their fruit, however, was at best inaccessible and probably also inedible if it existed in any meaningful way at all.

So we see that Jesus' comments on gardening are absolutely correct and don't require any qualification from RHS Wisley to understand. That is the superficial understanding of verse 44 – the middle verse of this short parable.

Verse 43 helps us get a bit closer to his underlying message: *"A good tree can't produce bad fruit, and a bad tree can't produce good fruit."* If the tree is sound, if the tree isn't diseased, if the tree produces flowers and blossom attractive to bees and insects, then it will produce fruit, good fruit. I know when my fruit trees produce good fruit because the birds and the wasps are all around them pecking and nibbling at the cherries and the apples until the fruit that remains is not quite so appetizing. But the tree hasn't produced bad fruit. If the fruit goes off because it's been eaten by birds and wasps, it is my fault, not the tree's or the fruit's or the birds'.

A good tree will produce good fruit given all the right conditions.

---

[7] Most congregations will have several people who will call out "fig trees" by this time.

A bad tree, however, will produce bad fruit. If the tree is diseased, that is likely to affect the fruit which may be damaged or not form properly.

As usual Jesus is not really talking about plants. Verse 45 makes it clear that we are meant to apply the same principle to people.

The previous section of his teaching has been about hypocrisy. Those who see it as their business to correct the faults of others should be careful to ensure that they have taken a good look at themselves first.

So take a good look at yourself; what kind of tree are you? What sort of fruit do you produce? Is it good fruit or bad fruit? To turn the question round a little bit, how do you know whether you're producing good fruit or bad fruit?

Jesus' next section about the wise and foolish builders is a bit of a clue. Those who are obedient to his words and his commands and to following in his ways are the ones who are good trees producing good fruit.

That's OK as far as it goes. But it only goes so far as the theory. I'm hoping you're still asking what that actually means in practice. There are two more passages that can help us take this a little further. Both are worth looking at in themselves and I'll do that with one of them in this book because it contains more of Jesus' comments about growing fruit. The other is a passage from St Paul.

Firstly, Jesus gave some help with how to be a good fruit tree in his comments that John records in his Gospel in chapter 15. For our purposes in connection with this passage it is enough to notice that Jesus says, *"I am the vine; you are the branches. Those who remain in me, and I in them, will produce much fruit. For apart from me you can do nothing."*

The way to be a good fruit tree and produce good fruit in obedience to Jesus is by remaining 'in him'. It means being connected to him, hearing from him, acting and thinking and speaking in accord with his ways. To continue the fruit tree analogy, it means having the sap from his root stock rising through your branches. It is his words and his ways that give you life. St Paul, in another passage that we might consider in greater depth if we were to look at 'Paul on Gardening', likens this to being grafted in. This is like a vine that will often have a branch from a particular kind of vine grafted on to another kind of root stock. To make the thinking human rather than horticultural, we could say that it is his breath you breathe; his ways are your ways so that you could say he lives in you.

That is precisely what we mean when we say that we have been given the Holy Spirit to live in us. Living by the Spirit, being led by the Spirit, being filled with the Spirit would be more traditional ways of saying that we're part of the same tree and would therefore be a good tree bearing good fruit.

That gets us some way to answering our questions about what sort of fruit we can expect to grow on our branches. But I think we can go a little bit further for those who are still saying, "Yes, but what does that fruit actually look like? How do I know I'm not out of my tree?"

This is where our other related passage comes in. In Galatians 5:22-23 Paul describes the fruit of the Spirit as *"love, joy, peace, patience, kindness, goodness, faithfulness, gentleness and self-control"*.

That's what the fruit of the Spirit is, that's what it's like, and that's how you can tell what sort of tree you are. You're a good tree, connected to Jesus' root stock and producing good fruit in obedience to his words and his ways if the fruit you bear has the characteristics of *"love, joy, peace, patience, kindness, goodness, faithfulness, gentleness and self-control"*.

That's not an exhaustive list but it does take in what characteristics you can expect to grow in you as you allow yourself to be led by the Spirit. In its context, that verse is telling us that the Spirit leading us produces those characteristics as opposed to the actions which flow from someone who is given over to following their own sinful desires.

I think it also indicates the characteristics that we might expect to see developing in people, places and situations around us when we take the Jesus kind of fruit tree into a place by our presence.

It is not an exhaustive list but it is also not a multiple choice list. This is not a case of the exam paper approach: attempt any three. It is not a matter of deciding that you'd like to be more loving and you'd like to see peace breaking out all around you in response to your words and actions, but you don't really want to be more gentle and you really don't think people around you should have any more joy and you're only prepared to have more patience if you can have it straight away.

The fruit that Jesus wants to see growing in us and around us is of one kind with these nine characteristics. So we know what kind of tree figs grow on and we know what kind of fruit grow on an apple tree. Now we can also say we know what kind of fruit grows on a Jesus tree. It's the love-joy-peace-patience-kindness-goodness-faithful-ness-gentleness-and-self-control fruit.

In colloquial speech now, just as much as in the first century, the heart is the centre of a person, the seat of the emotions and the source of all that comes out of us. In horticultural terms it is the roots. Jesus says:

> *"A good person produces good deeds from a good heart, and an evil person produces evil deeds from an evil heart. Whatever is in your heart determines what you say."*

So what kind of tree are you? What sort of fruit grows on your branches?

5

Jesus on Overproduction

The Parable of the Rich Fool

Luke 12:13-21

Someone in the crowd said to [Jesus], "Teacher, tell my brother to divide the inheritance with me." Jesus replied, "Man, who appointed me a judge or an arbiter between you?" Then he said to them, "Watch out! Be on your guard against all kinds of greed; life does not consist in an abundance of possessions." And he told them this parable: "The ground of a certain rich man yielded an abundant harvest. He thought to himself, 'What shall I do? I have no place to store my crops.' Then he said, 'This is what I'll do. I will tear down my barns and build bigger ones, and there I will store my surplus grain. And I'll say to myself, "You have plenty of grain laid up for many years. Take life easy; eat, drink and be merry." But God said to him, 'You fool! This very night your life will be demanded from you. Then who will get what you have prepared for yourself?' This is how it will be with whoever stores up things for themselves but is not rich towards God."

If you grow fruit or vegetables, you'll know what it is to have too much at once. At certain times in the season you find that all the lettuces or all the strawberries seem to have ripened or reached their optimum picking point at the same time. Our neighbours had that experience with cucumbers quite early in the season. Theirs are really nice, small cucumbers. The reason I know about this is not just because I've helped to water them later in the season in previous years. I know about their glut of cucumbers and the quality and size of them because of their solution to the problem of overproduction.

There are three things you can do if you have too many of something all at once. You can eat more than is good for you, leading to indigestion or gluttony. (There's a sermon in that but not out of this passage.) A second possibility would be the solution our neighbours chose; they gave some away – that's how I know what they were like. The third solution is to do what the rich man in Jesus' parable did; you can store them up, keep them for another day when there aren't so many to pick.

The method of storage, and its success, depends on the crop. We've still got blackberries in our freezer from some years ago, frozen within minutes of coming off the plant and they'll be good for puddings and jams for some time yet. We also store our surplus beans but they're best if you prepare them for cooking and blanche them – cook them for a short time and then freeze them. Some crops need to be kept in a dry environment. Grain crops would come into this category.

To store things, you usually have to do something to the crop. The E.U. (especially when it was the E.E.C.) demonstrates this. Over-production of grapes leads to a wine lake. Overproduction of grain leads to a grain mountain. So overproduction of milk leads to a milk – what?[8] The answer is "a milk mountain" because milk doesn't keep well as a liquid and has to be dried.

Cucumbers are more of a problem. They're not good frozen and you don't usually cook them. I tried pickling once but it wasn't very successful. Basically, if you've got too many of some crops, all you can do is pass them on. You either sell them or give them away. Our neighbours gave away their cucumbers and we're very grateful.

---

[8] Someone will probably say "lake" because milk is a liquid.

We're not told what sort of crops the man in Jesus' parable was growing but if he wanted to keep them in barns I expect they were in the dry storage category. What he has done is decide that his own efforts have given him security. It's the mentality that says, "I've worked hard all my life and I've made enough that I can put my feet up and enjoy myself." If you've worked hard, got a bit put by, invested well and contributed to a good pension scheme, you might be in this position.

You see we've already strayed on to Jesus' real point. As usual he's not talking about gardening or how to store your glut of fruit and vegetables. Jesus is talking about people. This time he's talking about our attitudes and what gives us security.

Many people have thought they'd got their retirement sorted out and discovered it was not so secure as they had believed or hoped. People who had invested heavily in property may have found that the credit crunch and the fall in property prices left them less well off than they expected. In retirement the short term is more important than the long term. It is all very well to say that property prices will always go up in the long term but if you were about to sell up and downsize and discovered that your house was not worth what you thought it was, the balance may not be enough to invest for the kind of income you hoped for.

This is especially true if stock markets and share prices are uncertain, or after bad news about a particular company.[9] It reminds me of the joke that went round during the credit crunch. Question: How do you make a small fortune these days? Answer: Start with a large one.

We're being encouraged to save, but if we do save, our savings don't grow because interest rates are virtually zero. So we're being encouraged to spend. Interestingly, in our context, *not* because we think our future is secure as the man in Jesus' parable did; oddly, we're being encouraged to spend in order to get the economy going again, but we have to do it with less money because of the cuts imposed so that we can live within our means as a country. It seems the government says spend while they're trying to save and tells us to

---

[9] There is often likely to be an up-to-date example of a company which has had bad results or adverse publicity which affected the share value.

spend more of the less that we have. There's something flawed about it somewhere but I can't see the way out.

Jesus' rich man has a large fortune and he decides that is his security. It is tied up in crops but presumably he is planning to sell them when he has need of income. If he has truly large amounts he will be an influential player in the supply market and so be able to control the price. He feels secure. So he says to himself, "I've made my pile" – pile of grain, vegetables or whatever – "so I can sit back, enjoy myself, eat drink and be merry."

Can you finish the quotation? "Eat, drink and be merry for..." Tomorrow you die. Cheerful, isn't it? But that is just about what Jesus says this man didn't think of. In this case it wasn't tomorrow, it was tonight. Jesus said that God posed the question to him, *"Then who will get it all?"* This is not really about inheritance. No doubt there would have been some way of avoiding inheritance tax, but the point is less about who would inherit, what they would get and how much would be left after tax and more about thinking about what's really important.

6

Jesus on Weed Killer

The Parable of the Weeds

Matthew 13:24-30;36-43

Jesus told them another parable: "The kingdom of heaven is like a man who sowed good seed in his field. But while everyone was sleeping, his enemy came and sowed weeds among the wheat, and went away. When the wheat sprouted and formed ears, then the weeds also appeared. The owner's servants came to him and said, 'Sir, didn't you sow good seed in your field? Where then did the weeds come from?' 'An enemy did this,' he replied. The servants asked him, 'Do you want us to go and pull them up?' 'No,' he answered, 'because while you are pulling up the weeds, you may uproot the wheat with them. Let both grow together until the harvest. At that time I will tell the harvesters: first collect the weeds and tie them in bundles to be burned; then gather the wheat and bring it into my barn.'"

I'm sure I heard a story of someone who had developed a strain of wheat that grew on short stalks. The obvious advantage of this to the farmer is that there is less waste in the form of straw and less likelihood of the wheat being top heavy and breaking before the harvest. This person went to someone and offered him seed for this short-stalked variety. The offer was refused; his potential business partner didn't want to try something different and didn't believe this was possible. Undaunted, the man with the new strain of wheat secretly sowed his seed in the field with the other wheat. When they came up, they grew together. From above it was possible to make out the words "told you" in shorter wheat across the field.

This story of Jesus is similar in that someone has sowed different seed secretly in a field. I imagine this enemy might have spelt out "ha ha" – or something similar. The farmer would have been able to see, as the two quite different plants came up together, that there were weeds among his wheat.

Context is so important with biblical stories like this. In so many ways they transfer cultures very easily, but in other ways we have to understand the differences because they wouldn't quite work today. Since the 1950s the question and its answer would have been different. A farm worker would not have been asking about pulling up the weeds. The question is more likely to have been about getting out the sprayer and using the weed killer. And with that kind of technology, the answer might well have been positive.

In Jesus' context weed killer was not possible. To remove a weed – a plant that is growing in the wrong place – you had to pull it out. There are innumerable jokes and stories about people who can't tell the difference between weeds and plants. I suppose the answer is that there isn't one. A weed is a plant; it's just not the plant that you happen to want to grow in that place. Jesus is not giving a lesson on telling the difference between weeds and plants. That is clearly a subjective judgment. If you want a patch of nettles rather than summer bedding, the 'weeds' are the petunias and the plants are the nettles – though it's usually the other way round.

Jesus' horticultural lesson is a bit more basic than that in this story. Here Jesus simply points out the dangers of trampling around amongst your crops trying to pull out plants you don't want from among the plants you do want when all the plants are young and tender. Quite apart from damaging the wheat as you try to get to the weeds there is the danger of uprooting wheat plants along with them. Do that and you end up with a reduced harvest.

These were days without selective weed killers; farming was not nearly so intense but it was just as important to maximize the harvest. So it is common sense to let the wheat grow to maturity and then deal with the weeds. It is easier to avoid uprooting wheat when it is full grown and if some is inadvertently pulled out with the weeds, it can be kept and added to the harvest.

As usual, none of this is Jesus' main point. It might be possible to make something of an environmental point and a horticultural point about the last verse of the section – verse 30 – *"collect the weeds and tie them in bundles to be burned"*. Burning is now not considered the best way to deal with weeds – composting would be much better because then they become useful in growing next year's crop. The further horticultural point could be that perennial weeds like dandelions should not be composted at home because they will come up in next year's crops. They should be taken to the council recycling facility where the compost will be sterilized before being used.

It does lead us, as perhaps this comment led Jesus' disciples for other reasons, to ask what this story is really all about. Remembering that, unlike us, they hadn't already read or heard the explanation when they heard it the first time around, this could easily be another of Jesus' rather cryptic comments that is clearly about more than gardening – but the question is, what is it really about?

Jesus was clearly in full flow and told another two stories before he finished and went indoors where his disciples could ask him about it. One of them is also a gardening story and we'll look at that another time. The other is more 'Jesus on Food' than 'Jesus on Gardening'. When they do get him by himself, the disciples are so puzzled by the parable about weeds and wheat that they ask Jesus to explain. Then we get the parallels that we're expecting:

Farmer = Son of Man – that is, Jesus himself.

Field = world.

Good seed = people of the kingdom.

Now that is interesting, because it might not be quite what we were expecting. We've seen the seed in another story as the word, the *message* of the kingdom that Jesus came to preach. Here the seed is the *people* of the kingdom. That's you and me, if we associate ourselves with Jesus, if we've heard his word and we're living as a force for the good things of the kingdom of heaven in the world around us.

Here the seed is the people, and the people of the kingdom will grow into plants that mature and bear fruit for the kingdom. It is imperative that they be allowed to grow and not be pulled out before their time.

The weeds = the people of the evil one.

Enemy = evil one – the devil.

Harvest = end of the age. That is the time when the Son of Man will come and gather in all those who are citizens of his kingdom to be with him for ever. There are other parables and stories that relate even more strongly to this aspect of harvest.

Harvesters = angels.

The weeds in the field with the wheat don't change the nature of the wheat, they don't turn it into something that is not intended to be there, but they do endanger the crop, they can choke the wheat and hide the wheat so that it doesn't bear the fruit it should. They cause sin and they do evil. Those sorts of plants are in the wrong place if they are among the plants that are doing the works of love, joy, peace, justice, truth and freedom. This world is meant to be a field full of the fruit of the kingdom and the Son of Man sows his seeds all over the field.

When the weeds are finally weeded out they are the sort of weeds that need to be burned, or composted by the Council where they can be sterilised.

In the meantime, there is one more message for those who are seeds sown by the Son of Man. If we look out and see that there are weeds in our part of the field, if it says "ha ha" in dandelions or mare's tail or ground elder across the field when we look out in the morning, then we need to be extra vigorous wheat plants to make sure that we grow on to maturity amid the competition.

If you look at the world and see violence, lies and self-interest and all that would direct people's attention away from God going on, then you need to work even harder at finding ways that you can grow into a person of life, peace, love, freedom, truth and justice, pointing people towards God and the ways of his kingdom.

7

Jesus on Growth (i)

The Parable of the Growing Seed

Mark 4:26-29

[Jesus] also said, "This is what the kingdom of God is like. A man scatters seed on the ground. Night and day, whether he sleeps or gets up, the seed sprouts and grows, though he does not know how. All by itself the soil produces corn – first the stalk, then the ear, then the full grain in the ear. As soon as the corn is ripe, he puts the sickle to it, because the harvest has come."

Most gardeners, and certainly any GCSE Biologist, would be able to fill in the ignorance of the man in Jesus' short story. This man may not know how it is that seeds sown in the ground grow up and form a mature plant with seed in its turn.

Whether the human Jesus, a first century Palestinian Jewish carpenter, would have known or whether this raises a question about Jesus also being the all-knowing second person of the Trinity is rather beside the point of the story.

Modern biology tells us about the action of light, moisture and warmth that triggers the growth in the seed so that it pushes shoots up through the ground towards the light. We now have some understanding of the codes in the DNA of the seed that mean it will produce a plant that is a replica of the parent.

As always with Jesus on gardening, he has another message for us. There is a sense in this story of inevitability. Whatever the man who sowed the seed does – whether he sleeps or gets up, whether he watches it or goes away, whether he takes action around it, talks to it, or ignores it – whatever he does or doesn't do, the seed grows.

The ignorance of Jesus' gardener about the process serves to underline this inevitability. This gardener doesn't know how his seeds grow; he doesn't seem to know what is good for them and will help them. He just sows the seeds and knows they will come up, grow strong, mature and bear fruit. This gardener's ignorance also gives a sense of mystery; whatever it is that Jesus is talking about is going to happen by some mysterious process that we don't – perhaps can't – understand.

The clue, as always, is in the context and the introduction. Mark puts this parable third in a series of four parables, three of which have a horticultural theme. The beginning of the chapter was the Parable of the Sower, or the Parable of the Soils, and its explanation. Next Mark recounts Jesus' teaching about the lamp which should be placed where it can be seen. Then, after this parable, comes the Parable of the Mustard Seed.

The Parable of the Sower was told while Jesus was teaching by the lake, in public in the open air where a large crowd gathered to hear. But after that Jesus went indoors with his disciples and gave them the explanation. So when Mark starts the section about the lamp on the stand he starts, *"[Jesus] said to them..."* 'Them' sounds as though it is the disciples. What he is saying in this section seems to be privileged information; it is for the insiders. At the end of the section[10] Mark tells us that with his disciples Jesus explained everything. It sounds as though the Parable of the Growing Seed may be part of an explanation! If it is, it still leaves some scope for mystery!

Following this application of the lamp on the stand image it may have something to do with the inevitability of the growth of God's kingdom. The lamp on the stand image in Mark 4 is not used to

---

[10] Mark 4:34

exhort his followers to let their good works be seen by everyone around. Nor is it about making sure our gifts and talents are not hidden by false modesty. The kingdom of God, as it comes into the world, shines a light into dark places and reveals them for what they are. The good, the bad and the ugly are shown up for what they are by the bright light of the kingdom. There is inevitability about it: *"Whatever is hidden is meant to be brought out into the open."*

So when the kingdom is planted in the world it will grow and bear fruit.

Our job, it seems from this parable, may have many facets. These are not incompatible but they do depend on slightly different interpretations.

Firstly, our role might be to plant, to sow seeds of the kingdom around us. That would mean being people of the kingdom, pursuing actions, attitudes and words that spread kingdom values and kingdom messages so that the sphere of God's rule is extended.

That means being people of peace where there is conflict and discord, seeking unity and harmony. It means being people of grace and forgiveness where there is an attitude of vengeance and grudge-bearing. It means being people of joy because of the eternal joy of God's presence and rule where there is sadness. It means being people of hope where there is despair and people of life where there is death and destruction.

With the sowing of such seeds in small ways in our own homes, families, workplaces, schools and local communities we can be confident that the kingdom will grow even though we don't know how it happens.

A second way to look at it might be that God has sown his seed of the kingdom in the world by sending Jesus. Once Jesus has come, preached his message of the nearness of the kingdom and fulfilled his mission through his death and resurrection, then the growth of the kingdom is inevitable and doesn't require God's actions. That leaves us with the responsibility to be the growing plants, to allow the seeds to bear fruit in us in words, actions and attitudes that reveal the kingdom.

Yet again it may be that once the seed of the kingdom is sown in us we can be confident that it will grow and bear fruit even though we don't really understand how it happens.

The Parable of the Mustard Seed that comes immediately after this parable lends support to the idea of the seed of the kingdom being sown in small ways and growing to maturity. If this whole section is part of Jesus' explanation of parables to his disciples, then the themes of the inevitability of the kingdom and its growth from small beginnings does seem to run through them. Similarly, if we take all four parables in the chapter together, it may be that when the word is sown, even as a tiny seed, in the good soil of people's lives it will grow and bear fruit in the ways, words, actions and attitudes of the kingdom in such a way that all will see it and be shown up in its light for what they are, whether good or evil.

8

Jesus on Growth (ii)

Mustard Seeds and Tree

Matthew 13:31-32; Mark 4:30-34; Luke 13:18-19

He told them another parable: "The kingdom of heaven is like a mustard seed, which a man took and planted in his field. Though it is the smallest of all seeds, yet when it grows, it is the largest of garden plants and becomes a tree, so that the birds come and perch in its branches."

Matthew 13:31-32

Again he said, "What shall we say the kingdom of God is like, or what parable shall we use to describe it? It is like a mustard seed, which is the smallest of all seeds on earth. Yet when planted, it grows and becomes the largest of all garden plants, with such big branches that the birds can perch in its shade." With many similar parables Jesus spoke the word to them, as much as they could understand. He did not say anything to them without using a parable. But when he was alone with his own disciples, he explained everything.

Mark 4:30-34

Then Jesus asked, "What is the kingdom of God like? What shall I compare it to? It is like a mustard seed, which a man took and planted in his garden. It grew and became a tree, and the birds perched in its branches.

Luke 13:18-19

When I was at university a rumour went round that while someone was visiting home for a weekend, his so called friends had sown mustard and cress seeds on his carpet and there was quite a respectable crop by the time he returned! Others, for whom life is too short for housework, might claim that you could grow mustard and cress in the dust! That's not the sort of mustard that Jesus was talking about! The seeds we use quite frequently with children's groups as illustration of growth are quite small but not as small as the seeds Jesus knew as mustard seeds. And while the seeds we sow grow rapidly up to several centimetres tall, they could not be described as a tree or even *"the largest of all garden plants".*

I used to think there was a large dose of 'rabbinic hyperbole' (exaggeration to make a point) in this parable of Jesus. Then I researched the subject and saw pictures of the kind of plant Jesus would have known as mustard towering above a man.

As a horticultural lesson, Jesus has provided this story to show that 'from tiny acorns grow mighty oaks' or the importance of providing shade and perches for the birds. It is notable that shade and perches can be provided for birds by planting very small seeds while also growing a useful crop for the gardener (if you like to use mustard).

This much is discernible from the shortest versions of the story and yet for the length of the story (only five verses in its longest version) there is more clue that as usual Jesus is not really speaking for gardeners. At the beginning of all three versions Jesus is explicit in stating the purpose of his story. He is drawing on gardening for an illustration of an aspect of the kingdom of God. *"The kingdom of heaven is like..." "What shall we say the kingdom of God is like?" "What is the kingdom of God like? What shall I compare it to?"*

Mark tells us that Jesus used many similar parables and didn't teach without using them. The implication is that this teaching in parables was addressed to the crowds who gathered to hear him because Mark also tells us that he explained everything to his disciples when they were alone. Perhaps this also implies that the disciples didn't always understand. As disciples we may need to understand that any one parable, even when decoded, doesn't explain the whole of the concept of the kingdom. Putting the three versions of the story together helps us to see what aspects are important to each evangelist. For Mark it is clear that it is important that we should notice how Jesus taught through stories that could be understood by his hearers but which also needed some explanation for his disciples. Luke simply tells the story, but even in just two verses almost labours the point that this is a comparison with the kingdom of God. Matthew also makes much of it being a parable and a comparison but emphasizes the extent of the growth.

From this horticultural story Jesus' disciples, both original and modern, may draw at least two simple lessons.

One may be put as the proverb quoted above: from tiny acorns grow mighty oaks. If only tiny examples of the kingdom are planted in a community or in people's hearts and minds, great things are possible if that tiny seed is watered and cared for. Even if you can only do little things for the kingdom in your neighbourhood or family it is still significant. The tiny seed grows into the largest of plants.

The second obvious point is the nature of the kingdom that grows from these small beginnings. When the plant has grown into a tree the branches provide perches and shade for the birds. As the kingdom extends its influence through a community there will be places and projects that provide shelter for people who are not part of the kingdom community but are drawn into its influence and benefits.

So a kingdom project that seeks to work for justice and freedom will benefit many who are not members of the church that set it up. A project that provides shelter for homeless people or a food bank will shelter many birds in its shady branches.

These influential projects and many like them all around the country often grow from tiny seeds of desire to make a difference in the minds of individuals. If you have a passion for a particular kingdom issue and a tiny seed of an idea about how to do something about it, you may be surprised at what God can do when he takes it and plants it in his field.

9

Jesus on Growth (iii)

When a Seed Dies

John 12:24

[Jesus said,] "Very truly I tell you, unless a kernel of wheat falls to the ground and dies, it remains only a single seed. But if it dies, it produces many seeds."

Taken as a verse on its own at face value, this is obvious, basic gardening or agricultural advice and information. Just to spell it out: if you're going to get more grain from a single grain of wheat you have to bury it in the ground. To all intents and purposes it has to die. When you do that – let go of it, let it fall to the ground and be of no use to you – only then do you give it a chance to live and grow and bear fruit in more grain – many seeds.

Take a grain of wheat – or any other seed for that matter, as St Paul adds in a similar piece of teaching in 1 Corinthians 15. Jesus just uses the example of wheat. So, take a grain of wheat and it is obvious that you have to put it in soil if you want it to grow and produce what grains of wheat produce when they grow. Most children in infant school have sown seeds like runner beans and watched for them to come up and grow into plants bearing fruit that eventually looks very like what they put in the soil in the first place.

So this isn't rocket science, though it does look like very basic biology. But Jesus didn't spend much time in his teaching on very basic biology (or rocket science). As always we need to put his saying in context.

If we put this one firstly in the context of his teaching in general, we conclude from his habit of speaking in parables that this piece of basic biology probably has a meaning that pointed people towards God, towards the spiritual side of life.

More specifically, this is John's Gospel and much of Jesus' teaching as John records it has to do with eternal life. A working hypothesis may be that this is about life more than death and perhaps the way to enter eternal life.

So, we've approached this verse through two layers of context: Jesus' teaching, and Jesus' teaching in John's Gospel. There's one further, more precise context to consider as well. This is from John chapter 12. What's been going on before Jesus comes out with this information?

The beginning of the chapter is when Jesus returned to Bethany, less than a week before Passover, and had dinner with Lazarus and his sisters Martha and Mary and many others who were following Jesus including the twelve disciples. There was also a large number of Jews including priests from Jerusalem.

At that dinner Mary took the opportunity to anoint Jesus with a large amount of expensive perfume and the fragrance filled the house. When controversy broke out with Judas Iscariot about the use of resources, especially financial resources, Jesus started talking about death – specifically his own death. That seems like a bit of a leap, but Jesus often does that, going from a seemingly material or worldly topic of conversation to a rather different topic, often a spiritual one, in one easy step which seems to us more like crunching the gears.

Jesus told them that this perfume was being saved for his burial. Spices and strong-smelling perfumes were used at burial to overcome something of the odours of dead bodies. Jesus simply said that she'd done this while he was still alive and the action pointed towards his death; the implication being that this event was not far off.

John also makes a point of referring to Lazarus having been raised from the dead. Death is 'in the air' in this passage. The events at the beginning of that chapter took place in the home of a man who had died – and been raised from the dead. Death is hard to avoid in this context. Death is a strong topic of conversation in this chapter.

The chief priests go off to plot how to put Jesus to death and have Lazarus killed as well. But we've still not quite reached this verse about grains of wheat.

The following day – now just five days before Passover – Jesus goes to Jerusalem and is greeted by crowds who turn the event into something resembling the triumphant return of a king.

But even in this event John gets in a reference to Jesus' death. John says that his disciples made the connection between this event and some Old Testament prophecies. But they didn't make the connection until after Jesus was glorified. When John writes of Jesus' glorification he is referring to the crucifixion at least as much as the resurrection and ascension. And then John squeezes in another reference to Lazarus being raised from the dead and the impact this had on the crowds who followed Jesus because of it.

All through the chapter John has been sliding in references to death – especially Jesus' death. He's also been referring to resurrection, especially by way of Lazarus. The whole chapter seems to be about how life in Jesus' economy comes after death.

So Jesus gets to Jerusalem and John records the slightly curious incident of some Greeks who want to see Jesus but seem to need a disciple to take them to him. They approach Philip probably because he has a Greek name. It then seems slightly odd that Philip doesn't feel able to take them to Jesus by himself and asks Andrew to help him. We're not told what the Greeks wanted but we might assume that they weren't there wondering how to get some grain, or what to do with a grain of wheat. These Greeks were not in Jerusalem for a biology lesson or to find an agricultural college.

Andrew and Philip take these Greeks – non-Jews, but ones who were there for the festival, so God-fearers – to see Jesus, and Jesus replies, *"Very truly I tell you, unless a kernel of wheat falls to the ground and dies, it remains only a single seed. But if it dies, it produces many seeds."*

It's another example of Jesus sliding seamlessly from one topic of conversation to another in order to press home his spiritual point. This single sentence, dressed up as simple gardening advice, presses home the point he's been making at every opportunity at least since the raising of Lazarus in chapter 11.

Coming to eternal life – real life, life in all its fullness, life as a citizen of the kingdom of God – involves a death. His concentration on his own death indicates that is the death he is really talking about. The raising of Lazarus was a sign that life comes from death and many people followed him because of it. But the signs usually point to Jesus. Associated with each one is an "I am..." saying. When Jesus raised Lazarus from the dead he told Martha, *"I am the Resurrection and the Life."*

So the grain of wheat that falls to the ground and dies is Jesus himself; the seed, though apparently dead, comes to life and behaves as it was created to be – it produces more seed, more grain.

It is Jesus' death, and his resurrection life that follows it, that produces in us the eternal life of the kingdom. We follow him and we can be like him and live his life because he died and rose to show that death is not the end, not final, not all there is.

10

Jesus on Finds in the Garden

The Parable of the Hidden Treasure

Matthew 13:44

[Jesus said,] "The kingdom of heaven is like treasure hidden in a field. When a man found it, he hid it again, and then in his joy went and sold all he had and bought that field."

We used to be avid watchers of Time Team on Channel 4. We'd enjoy seeing them doing geophysics across an apparently bare field and interpreting various black splodges as walls, post holes, rooms and so on. And then we'd watch with anticipation as they took the turf off to start Trench One and scrape away with trowels to uncover tiny fragments of bone from ancient rubbish tips. Sometimes this digging would uncover larger fragments of cooking pots or high status drinking vessels or plates from a Roman Villa, or even valuable jewellery. The computer generated graphics would rebuild the best of the original items so viewers could see what they might have looked like. An artist would draw scenes of the most important historical moments from the past life of the area or house incorporating what they had discovered and some of the pieces they'd found.

One year, Time Team ran a project called The Big Dig to get viewers digging in their gardens, and we registered with enthusiasm.

All we had to do was dig a one metre square test pit up to one metre deep in ten centimetre levels. That dig didn't actually uncover anything of any value, though we do have several pieces of iron and pot, and photos of each stage of the dig. We lived in a vicarage built in the 1960s in the garden of a much older house. Our garden included the area that had been the stable yard and greenhouse of the old house. We chose where to dig hoping to find more of the flooring of some of those buildings.

In previous years we had developed that part of the garden and found a cobbled floor divided into several bays next to the garden wall. We were really pleased with that and so proud of our find that we altered our plans to incorporate one of those bays as a sunken area between two areas of planting. I hope you get some idea of what it was like!

The point is that sometimes we find things in the garden that we're really pleased with. They take us by surprise, or they're interesting or historic, or they turn out to be useful or even sometimes valuable. When that happens we behave differently from the way we do when all we turn up is stones and bits of the plastic flower pot we broke last year or pieces of polystyrene from the bedding plant containers.

I imagine Jesus might have had something similar in mind when he told this one-verse parable.[11]

Presumably the man in Jesus' story was digging in a field as a labourer, turning the soil over, maybe planting plants or simply digging out stones or weeds to make a finer soil for seeds. He came unexpectedly upon buried treasure. Time Team sometimes visited places where artefacts were easier to turn up because ploughing over the years had disturbed the soil over long-buried objects. Perhaps this is what had happened for the man in Jesus' parable. The point is similar to our archaeological finds in the garden: he behaved differently from the way he would have done if all he had uncovered were stones and animal bones.

The human, psychological point is that when we discover something of value to us we do what we can to make it ours. So, even though the vicarage garden and the remains of its associated

---

[11] This could be a good point in the sermon to reiterate the parable.

outbuildings could never really belong to us, we did what we could to make it ours. We developed the garden in our own way, incorporating and showing off our find. There is a bit of a stamp of Muskett on that garden until or unless someone decides to cover it all up again!

The man in Jesus' parable also wanted to make the discovery his own. The field and its contents didn't belong to him so he couldn't just take the treasure away. As soon as he was seen to be so much better off, it would come out where he'd acquired his newfound riches and he'd be accused of stealing. This man had to acquire the treasure honestly so he sold all he had to get enough money together to buy the field. That way any contents would legally be his.

We might want to question whether that was a bit underhand and not entirely honest but I think that is simply the point at which we find we've stretched Jesus' parallels too far. As usual with Jesus' stories, he is not really talking about human activity such as digging in fields or even garden archaeology. He is using ideas and activities that we and his hearers can understand and perhaps identify with in order to convey something spiritual.

As with so many of Jesus' parables, the clue as to what he's really talking about is in the introduction: *"The kingdom of heaven is like..."*

In this case the kingdom is likened to the treasure. It is hidden but it is very close to us; we can come across it in the course of our everyday activity but that discovery may well be unexpected.

Discovery of the kingdom unexpectedly within reach prompts the one who finds it to do all in his power to make it his, to come into that kingdom. When we find something valuable in the garden we do what we can to clean it up and show it off as ours. When we find the kingdom we do what we can to grasp it, make it ours and ensure our place in it.

This man *"sold all he had and bought the field"*. He invested everything in it. The kingdom is something of such value that it is worth putting our whole selves into becoming part of it.

It doesn't mean we should sell everything we have – there are other passages that might imply that, though I don't think they necessarily mean that either. But it does mean that we should catch ourselves and think again if we're ever tempted to feel that anything we have, any of our possessions, any of our property or our 'stuff' is of comparable value to our place in the kingdom of heaven.

Discovering that we can live eternally with God in a place of love and peace, justice and joy because all that keeps us away from him has been dealt with in Jesus fills us with such overwhelming joy and delight that we immediately put everything into being a part of that eternal kingdom both in the here and now and on into eternity.

The point of this parable is of such importance that Jesus pushes it home by telling another very similar story based on a different context. Verses 45 and 46 are set in the world of a businessman who deals in fine pearls and discovers one that is finer than anything he could imagine:

"Again, the kingdom of heaven is like a merchant looking for fine pearls. When he found one of great value, he went away and sold everything he had and bought it."

11

Jesus on the Workforce (ii)

Recruitment and Pay

Matthew 20:1-16

"For the kingdom of heaven is like a landowner who went out early in the morning to hire workers for his vineyard. He agreed to pay them a denarius for the day and sent them into his vineyard. About nine in the morning he went out and saw others standing in the market-place doing nothing. He told them, 'You also go and work in my vineyard, and I will pay you whatever is right.' So they went. He went out again about noon and about three in the afternoon and did the same thing. About five in the afternoon he went out and found still others standing around. He asked them, 'Why have you been standing here all day long doing nothing?' 'Because no one has hired us,' they answered. He said to them, 'You also go and work in my vineyard.' When evening came, the owner of the vineyard said to his foreman, 'Call the workers and pay them their wages, beginning with the last ones hired and going on to the first.' The workers who were hired about five in the afternoon came and each received a denarius. So when those came who were hired first, they expected to receive more. But each one of them also received a denarius. When they received

it, they began to grumble against the landowner. 'These who were hired last worked only one hour,' they said, 'and you have made them equal to us who have borne the burden of the work and the heat of the day.' But he answered one of them, 'I am not being unfair to you, friend. Didn't you agree to work for a denarius? Take your pay and go. I want to give the one who was hired last the same as I gave you. Don't I have the right to do what I want with my own money? Or are you envious because I am generous?' So the last will be first, and the first will be last."

When it was introduced there was much debate about the rightness of the minimum wage. Since then there has been debate about how much it should be, whether it should go up and so on. There is currently debate about Government programmes designed to help people get back into a 'work habit' or develop a lifestyle and routine compatible with work after a long period of unemployment. These schemes have been criticised as taking advantage and of giving companies a cheap workforce when they could afford to take on staff properly and pay at least the minimum wage. The minimum wage in our culture is an hourly rate. It seems that in the kingdom of God it will be a daily rate. At one time, anti-poverty campaigners talked about those who had to live on a dollar a day. In the kingdom of God, according to this parable of Jesus, it seems no one will be required to live on less than a denarius a day.

In this parable Jesus perhaps indicates that the daily rate in the kingdom of God is a bit like car parking charges. Just as you pay for up to two hours even if you only need forty-five minutes, so in the kingdom of God you get a denarius a day even if you only work an hour. This is not actually about how we pay our gardeners. It seems to indicate that if your gardener works for a day you should pay that daily rate and if your gardener only works an hour you should still pay the daily rate.

On the face of it this parable is about fairness and it demonstrates what a slippery ethic fairness is. Is it fair to reward someone who has worked one hour the same as those who have worked for eight? Is it fair to expect someone to live on only an eighth of a denarius a day just because for some unknown but possibly very good or even heart-wrenching reason they were unable to get to the recruitment point before 9 o'clock in the morning? Is it fair to tell a vineyard owner that he cannot negotiate a contract at any point during the grape-picking season with whatever workers are available? Is it fair to expect a vineyard owner to pay bonuses above the agreed wage when that is not part of the contract just because he has negotiated a vague contract to 'pay what is right' to others who joined the workforce later? How, in any employment situation, do you work out a fair wage?

If this parable is about fairness, especially in employment relations, then its most obvious point is that fairness is a difficult concept to pin down and one person's fairness is another's favouritism and another's exploitation.

This parable is a longer story at the end of a series of incidents and stories that feature wealth and coming into the kingdom. It looks as though Jesus wants to underline his teaching and get us to see what God is like and the way he treats wealth when it comes to entry into the kingdom. Like the previous piece of teaching at the end of chapter 19, Jesus ends this story with the phrase, *"The last will be first and the first shall be last."*

So if this parable is about the fairness of entering the kingdom, it seems that fairness is defined by the one that permits entrance not by those who seek it. The vineyard owner decides who gets to work in the vineyard and what their reward shall be. It is not for those who have been Christians all their lives and worked hard in so many ways for God and his church, perhaps in times and places that are very difficult, to criticise the Lord who gives as good a place in his kingdom to the person in her nineties who comes to Christ after her active days are past.

That seems to be about as far as fairness goes in this parable but there are a number of other points to notice. In terms of market gardening or farming there is something here about recruitment. This vineyard owner is aware of a need for a labour force; he knows there is a job to do for several people.

Actually we're not told at what point in the year this story is set. Perhaps we most naturally think of harvest time; this owner doesn't want to waste his crop – the harvest needs to be got in before it rots on the vine. But it could be that he's just planting his vineyard and wants to make sure the young vines get in the ground before they dry out. Or maybe it's pruning time and the job needs to be done before the sap starts rising to ensure good, clean vines with strong, healthy new shoots where the grapes will form.

Whatever it is, the vineyard owner knows he needs a workforce and he does what he needs to do to recruit. He goes out early to where the casual workforce waits around for someone to hire them and he takes on as many as he can find who will go. We don't know whether that was not enough or whether he just felt a few more wouldn't hurt but he goes out again and again to see if there are any more seeking work. He even goes out just an hour before the end of the working day.

I don't think this is about a desperate need to get the job done. It could have been that he'd planned very badly and the job had to be finished that day, but that's not the impression I get of this vineyard owner, the way Jesus tells the story.

I also don't think this is a message for twenty-first century gardeners to reassure us that it doesn't matter what time of day you do your gardening.

As usual with Jesus, I think this is a story to show us something of the heart of God. The kingdom of God is like... The kingdom of God is like a vineyard owner who... In the kingdom, when we see the kingdom in action, when we can know that the kingdom of God is near we will see the attitudes of the vineyard owner in practice.

This vineyard owner wants to give everyone a chance to be part of his workforce. This vineyard owner hates to see people standing around with nothing to do and therefore nothing to live on. This vineyard owner takes every opportunity to invite people to come in and join up with him and work to produce the fruit of his vineyard. This vineyard owner doesn't set out to be fair – except in so far as everyone has a chance to work for him. He doesn't set out to be fair - he sets out to be generous.

God welcomes people into his kingdom at any time; he seeks people out at all stages and times of their lives. God rewards a lifetime's labour in his service with an eternal place in his kingdom; he rewards a few years' labour in his service with an eternal place in his kingdom.

To pick up Tom Wright's translation of the last verse of this parable:

We shouldn't give God the evil eye because he is good; just because God's goodness is greater than ours and his generosity far in excess of ours doesn't mean we can accuse him of unfairness. Life isn't fair – no one ever said it would be. But God is fair – his mercy and justice, his love and compassion and his generosity is available for all at all time and in all places.

12

Jesus on Horticulture Failures

The Cursed Fig Tree

Matthew 21:18-22; Mark 11:12-14,20-26

Early in the morning, as [Jesus] was on his way back to the city, he was hungry. Seeing a fig tree by the road, he went up to it but found nothing on it except leaves. Then he said to it, "May you never bear fruit again!" Immediately the tree withered. When the disciples saw this, they were amazed. "How did the fig tree wither so quickly?" they asked. Jesus replied, "Truly I tell you, if you have faith and do not doubt, not only can you do what was done to the fig tree, but also you can say to this mountain, 'Go, throw yourself into the sea,' and it will be done. If you believe, you will receive whatever you ask for in prayer."

We've had some horticultural failures in our time; beans that produced hardly any fruit, tomatoes that got blight and so on. We had a verbascum that was a very poor specimen in one garden but which did really well when we moved it to another – until I used it as an illustration or parable of people needing the right conditions in which to thrive. After that it died completely. But we've never had a plant that we could get rid of by cursing it – not even (or perhaps especially not) dandelions! Conversely, and more productively, we've never had a plant that we could make do well – grow, thrive and produce fruit – simply by talking to it.

We do have a couple of fig trees; small ones which we grow in pots that are far more ornamental than they are productive. We over-winter them in the greenhouse and they do produce fruit but we've only ever had two figs that we picked when ripe to eat. We get leaves and embryonic fruit but we haven't been careful enough to select the fruit for next year, prune and protect it over the winter or feed it sufficiently during the summer.

This account of Jesus' reaction to a fig tree without fruit always seems a bit strange. It is strange enough in Matthew's account where we have to work out that it was springtime because it was just before Passover and therefore figs should not be expected. But it is even more strange in Mark. In this instance it is not so much 'Jesus on Gardening' as 'Mark on Gardening'. Mark points out what Jesus didn't seem to know:

Seeing in the distance a fig-tree in leaf, he went to find out if it had any fruit. When he reached it, he found it had nothing but leaves, because it was not the season for figs.[12]

Jesus' reaction to curse the tree that it would never again bear fruit always seems to me to be unreasonable and extreme. But I can't leave it there. I can't believe that something so apparently peculiar and irrational about Jesus can have made it into the Bible – twice – and not have something to teach us. So I find myself asking (as so often), "What's that all about then?"

As usual, I don't think that what it teaches us is very much to do with gardening.

The simplest form of the story is in Matthew. In this account it is the Monday of Holy Week, the day after Palm Sunday, and Jesus is returning to the city having spent the night at Bethany. It seems that Jesus wanted to be up and doing early, and Martha and Mary, if that's whom he was staying with, hadn't provided breakfast before he went. As he was on the way he felt hungry and was naturally upset that a potential source of food was not available.

---

[12] Mark 11:13 (NIV)

It's tempting to wonder whether this is about Jesus always being ahead of us and our expectations. Here he is too early in the day for breakfast and too early in the year for figs. But I don't think that explanation really works because it doesn't connect with anything he says about it.

Matthew tells us very simply that Jesus cursed the fig-tree and it withered immediately causing understandable amazement in his disciples. I imagine three facets to their amazement. Firstly, and most obviously, amazement that the fig tree withered just by being told never again to bear fruit. Secondly, that Jesus was so cross with it for not having fruit out of season that his reaction was to curse it. And thirdly, that if he could do that and he was hungry, as presumably they were too, why didn't he tell it to produce some figs so they could all have breakfast?

The way Matthew tells it, this incident seems to be about the prayer of faith. Jesus' reply begins, *"Truly..."*; a sure sign that he's spotted a teaching opportunity and wants them to understand something. *"Truly I tell you, if you have faith and do not doubt, not only can you do what was done to this fig tree..."*

It brings us face to face with the nature of faith and doubt. Many people have prayed for things more serious and positive than breakfast for those who couldn't wait for their B&B hosts to provide it. But this seems to be based on anger or pique. Many people have prayed for things apparently far more serious, far more deserving and far more productive and positive than this and their requests have not been granted. It is tempting but insensitive, unhelpful and arrogant to say that they clearly didn't have enough faith, or perhaps they doubted that God could or would really provide for them. Obviously, Jesus being the second person of the Trinity means that he could have no doubts about God's actions, whatever he asked for.

I hope you're shouting at me now that while it seems reasonable, that last sentence doesn't really hold water. "What about Gethsemane?" you should be asking. Well, we'll come to that in more detail in chapter 17 but that is certainly the most obvious point at which Jesus is not confident that what he wants is necessarily the same as what God wants. In Gethsemane Jesus is saying that what he wants is that what he wants should be what God wants but actually what he wants seems to be not what God wants! He prays for the cup of suffering to be taken from him but only if that is God's will.

I think that might be a bit of a clue to this strange case of the withering fig tree. Presumably this was a wild fig tree, not cultivated by anyone for their food. No one was dependent on it. Jesus may have been hungry but none of them so desperately hungry that they couldn't wait until they got to Jerusalem to contribute to the local economy and buy something. This was within God's will partly because no one was adversely affected by the withering of this fig tree and partly because this was a good time and place for the disciples to have a revision session about prayer and the works and power of God.

It was the right time because it was the beginning of Holy Week, the situation was becoming tense and critical, matters would soon be coming to a head with the Jewish authorities after the carnival atmosphere of Palm Sunday and they needed to know that they could rely on God and put their faith and trust in him for anything.

I think we have a clue to it being the right place as well from the rest of Jesus' reply, not quoted earlier. When the disciples asked how the fig tree had withered so quickly Jesus replied:

"Truly I tell you, if you have faith and do not doubt, not only can you do what was done to this fig tree, but also you can say to this mountain, 'Go throw yourself into the sea,' and it will be done." (NIV)

This mountain... *Which* mountain? Well, they're on their way to Jerusalem from Bethany so there are number of possibilities.

Jesus could have meant the Mount of Olives but there's nothing that really leads us to think that.

Jesus could have meant Mount Zion – the Temple Mount – and given his treatment of the money changers and sellers of doves he could have been cross enough. But that would be uprooting the central focus of the Jewish religion. It would have been tantamount to saying that with faith you could tell God to remove himself from his people. That only fits with Jesus coming as God among his people after he has completed that work and made the Temple as the focus of God's presence redundant by his presence. Also, if this had been clearly what Jesus meant I imagine there would have been some comment of amazement and lack of understanding, even shock and horror from the disciples. This is, after all, the Jesus who said that he came not to replace the law but to fulfil it. In a sense the Temple needs to remain to be superseded, not thrown out to be replaced.

The third possibility is that Jesus meant the mountain known as the Herodian. This was a mountain where Herod had built a palace but a mountain that was of human construction. Many people had laboured for many years to construct a mountain that would have been visible on Jesus' route into Jerusalem from Bethany. It seems to me that Jesus is saying that God's power is so much greater than that of the human rulers that, with a word, the faith that accords with God's work can accomplish so much more than human beings labour over.

All of that is in both Matthew's account and Mark's account. I've concentrated on Matthew because it is simpler and all together. But Mark does present it differently and I think there are lessons to be learnt from his presentation. Mark's order of events is different. Jesus enters Jerusalem on Palm Sunday but after a look around goes back to Bethany for the night.[13] On the way back in the morning Jesus curses the fig tree in the hearing of his disciples and without comment they go into Jerusalem.[14] In Jerusalem Jesus throws the money changers out of the Temple provoking anger and resentment in the chief priests and teachers of the law and amazement in the crowd.[15] Jesus and his disciples go out of the city[16] and it is only on their return the following day (Tuesday) that they notice that the fig tree has withered, and receive Jesus' (slightly extended) revision lesson on prayer in response to Peter's comment.[17]

Perhaps this positioning of the fig tree incident around the cleansing of the Temple is meant to help us with our interpretation.

If Jesus sees the old ways of religion, the people God has chosen, as no longer bearing fruit (the fig tree) or as putting material gain at the expense of others before a proper worship and reverence at the presence of God (the Temple), it may be that the cursing of the fig

---

[13] Mark 11:1-11
[14] Mark 11:12-14
[15] Mark 11:15-18
[16] Mark 11:19
[17] Mark 11:20-26

tree is an acted parable in a similar way to the cleansing of the Temple.

The cleansing of the Temple is about the true coming of God among his people. Cleansing the court of the Gentiles means that worship and access to the presence of God is opened up to all. Material gain should not be at the expense of people's access to the place of prayer and worship. Jesus comes to remove the corrupt ways that impede worship and restore the true presence of God.

Coming either side of the cleansing of the Temple, the cursing of the fig tree also stands for the rejection of the unfruitful ways of religion and worship and their replacement with the true vine, the branches of which are pruned to bear maximum fruit.[18]

This interpretation perhaps lends weight to the idea that the mountain Jesus meant was indeed the Temple Mount. If you have the kind of faith that withers a fig tree with a word, meaning that the religion of the Temple no longer produces fruit, then you can equally say to the Temple Mount that it should be uprooted and thrown into the sea as it is replaced as the focus of the presence of God by the presence of Jesus himself.

The lesson on prayer seems to be the same from both Matthew and Mark but Mark interestingly includes verses 25 and 26 on forgiveness which Matthew leaves out. Forgiveness, as an attitude to anyone you hold anything against, seems to sit slightly awkwardly with cursing a fig tree for not bearing fruit out of season but it is consistent with Jesus' teaching on prayer and our relationships with one another. Our relationships and attitudes to one another seem to be related very closely to our relationship with God. This verse seems to be Mark's version of the teaching that Matthew and Luke put into the Lord's Prayer: "Forgive us our debts (or sins) in the same way as we forgive our debtors (or those who sin against us)."

Jesus seems to take an opportunity to reiterate this teaching the day after he has witnessed anger, resentment, envy and a plot to kill him. At this point the disciples don't know quite how far this is to be taken but it will become clear at the end of the week when Jesus prays, *"Father, forgive them, they do not know what they are doing."*

---

[18] John 15

13

Jesus on the Workforce (iii)

Family Firm

Matthew 21:28-32

[Jesus said], "What do you think? There was a man who had two sons. He went to the first and said, 'Son, go and work today in the vineyard.' 'I will not,' he answered, but later changed his mind and went. Then the father went to the other son and said the same thing. He answered, 'I will, sir,' but he did not go. Which of the two did what his father wanted?" "The first," they answered. Jesus said to them, "Truly I tell you, the tax collectors and the prostitutes are entering the kingdom of God ahead of you. For John came to you to show you the way of righteousness, and you did not believe him, but the tax collectors and the prostitutes did. And even after you saw this, you did not repent and believe him."

Many parents will have had the same experience as the man in Jesus' story. Ask a teenager to do something and he or she is going to give one of two reactions. Either a very willing "yes, or course I will" – especially if you're offering to pay. Or a sullen "no, I can't be bothered, I've got better things to do" – which probably means they expect more pay than you're offering.

So how does a father get the garden done without either spending all his leisure hours out there while the rest of the family is indoors with their feet up watching television or paying over the odds to get someone in when there are perfectly healthy offspring to hand?

Jesus is surprisingly silent about the answer to that question. So anyone wanting some help with that will need to look elsewhere.

He does, however, point out that teenagers' responses to requests can be quite different from their actions. One who sounds willing may prove easily distracted. One who seems sullen and disengaged may prove unexpectedly helpful. What people say may be quite different from what they actually do. Perhaps the only clue we get from Jesus for getting the gardening jobs done is to have two children in the hope that one will help even if it's the one who said they wouldn't!

That's probably as much as we can hope to get about gardening – or running the family firm – from this parable. As usual with Jesus, there must be more to it. If he's not really talking about gardening, what is he talking about?

Most bibles put a heading at the top of this story that says something like "The Parable of the Two Sons". That helpfully points out what is obvious once we read it and may help us to find what we're looking for but unhelpfully it breaks up the narrative of the Gospel meaning that we lose sight of the fact that this story comes in a context. Most of Jesus' teaching comes in parables and is usually prompted by a comment or a question.

Sometimes the prompt is included in the chapter or the passage under the heading of the parable. By way of example, Luke 15 contains three parables where something or someone has gone missing. The chapter begins with Pharisaic criticism of the attention Jesus gave to tax collectors and sinners – those who were outside the orthodox religious definition of the kingdom of God; those who were 'lost'.

The section containing this Parable of the Two Sons simply begins with Jesus telling a story. It is clearly a story with a point because he starts, *"What do you think?"* But we have to look above the heading (which wasn't in Matthew's original document) to see why he might be telling this story at this time. Who's he telling it to? What do we suppose they might be expected to think?

In the section before, Jesus was in the Temple courts on the Monday of Holy Week – the day after Palm Sunday – according to Matthew's timescale. This is the day sometimes known as the 'day of questions'. The chief priests and elders came to Jesus while he was teaching and asked about his authority for what he was doing. They may have meant whether he had authority to teach in the Temple Courts. They may have been referring to his actions the day before in overturning the tables of the money changers.

It is recorded in numerous places that Jesus taught as one who had authority. It seems that it was clear from what he said and the way that he said it that his teaching was from God. He taught the ways of God and was not swayed by the status of his listeners or questioners.

Similarly, his actions had the stamp of authority and integrity about them as well. What he did backed up the teaching about what God requires. He acted justly, loved mercy and walked humbly before God.[19]

Whatever their motivation, it was a clear attempt to get him turned out either for not having any authority or for claiming too much by making some claim to have the direct authority of God. Jesus, as usual, is a step ahead of them. He makes use of a typical rabbi's technique.

Question: Why does a rabbi answer one question with another?
Answer: Why not?

Jesus asks them about the origins of John the Baptist's baptism. It was fairly clear to everyone that John was a messenger in the tradition of the Old Testament prophets who brought a word from God that was a challenge to the people to "return to the Lord" and demonstrate their turning by being baptised. Baptism was symbolic of turning away from the ways of corruption and deceit and their self-seeking and lack of care for others, being washed clean in God's sight and welcomed into the kingdom. This much was obvious.

But the chief priests and elders can't say categorically it was from God because they didn't take any notice. There were not apparently any mass baptisms of chief priests and elders by John. Nor can they say categorically that John's baptism was all the invention of his own

---

[19] Micah 6:8

charismatic personality in order to get a following and so definitively of no spiritual worth at all. The people all believed John was a prophet and responded accordingly.

So Jesus has them in a bind. If they can see but not admit to what is obvious about John the Baptist, they can probably see but won't admit to what is obvious about Jesus and his authority. Jesus draws the parallel and lets them see their own hypocrisy.

If we ignore the paragraph heading in the Bible, the text goes like this:

> *Jesus said, "Neither will I tell you by what authority I am doing these things. What do you think? There was a man who had two sons..."* [20]

The parable is designed to make the same point. Having stuck the knife in, he twists it with a fairly innocuous story about staffing the family vineyard. He lures them into the trap again with a question to which the answer is obvious. This is the kind of thing I remember doing in English Comprehension at Junior School. You read a passage and answer the questions. The answers are in the text. The test is simply to see whether you can understand what you read.

They should have known from the start that it was about God and his people because it was a story about a vineyard. That should have had sufficient Old Testament reference to be a clear signal that this could be about who's in and who's out of God's kingdom.

The question is simply about which of the sons does as he's asked. Which one is obedient to his father? Who among the people are actually doing what the owner of the vineyard asks of them?

This time the chief priests and elders can't say they don't know the answer because it is a direct comprehension question. You can almost hear them thinking, "Well, duh!" Of course the one who did what his father wanted was the one who went and did the work even if he had said he wouldn't – the one who was asked first in the story, as it happens.

If you can imagine the "Well, duh!" you can certainly hear that they almost didn't make it to the end of the answer, "The fi-i-i-i-irst," as they realised that Jesus was twisting the knife.

---

[20] Matthew 21:27-28 (NIV)

Who are the ones who responded to John's call to baptism and enter the kingdom of heaven because they have returned to the ways of the Lord? Who are the ones who are responding to his teaching and entering the kingdom of heaven because they have returned to the ways of the Lord? The tax collectors and the prostitutes.

The tax collectors and the prostitutes. The ones who don't say the right things, the ones who are regarded as outcast and excluded by the more respectable people. But they enter the kingdom of heaven because they do what God requires: they turn, they repent, they give back dishonest gains, repay what they've cheated and sit at Jesus' feet, hear his teaching and follow him, providing for his needs.

Who are the ones who say all the right things but don't lift a finger to help those in need under their noses? Who are the ones who make a big show of keeping the minutiae of the law but find ways of wriggling out of the major commandments like honouring their parents? Who are the ones who stand on street corners to pray in their ostentatious prayer shawls and attend Temple sacrifices every day but support the buying and selling of doves and pigeons in the court of Gentiles so others can't get near to worship? The chief priests and the elders.

The chief priests and the elders are the son who says he'll go and work in the vineyard, but rather than do God's works of mercy, they make insignificant sacrifices out of their wealth; rather than pursue justice for the poor and elderly, they set aside their wealth for the already wealthy Temple and deny any help to parents, to widows and orphans or strangers among the community.

Jesus brings it back to John as he points all this out at the end of the story. John had given this message; John had referred them to the prophets who spoke of God requiring mercy not sacrifice; God requiring mercy, justice and humility. They'd heard John, they'd seen the response and still they were unmoved. Why should he give them an answer about his authority when it was just as obvious?

It doesn't help us get our children to work in the garden but this story does reinforce the point for me that when God asks us to go and work in the vineyard it is better to get on and do it than to make a big thing of what working in the vineyard involves but not actually do it.

That's clearly a challenge to the preacher and the professionally religious but also to all of us to keep before us the prophetic statement that what the Lord requires is *"to act justly, love mercy and walk humbly before your God"*. Blessed are those, Jesus said, who hear the word of God and obey it.

14

Jesus on Fruit Trees (ii)

Productivity

Luke 13:6-9

Jesus told this parable: "A man had a fig-tree growing in his vineyard, and he went to look for fruit on it but did not find any. So he said to the man who took care of the vineyard, 'For three years now I've been coming to look for fruit on this fig-tree and haven't found any. Cut it down! Why should it use up the soil?' 'Sir,' the man replied, 'leave it alone for one more year, and I'll dig round it and fertilise it. If it bears fruit next year, fine! If not, then cut it down.'"

We've had a couple of fig trees for quite a few years which we grow in pots and take into the greenhouse over winter. Figs like to have their roots restricted and they don't want to get too cold, especially not round the roots, so we're giving them quite a good chance. They often have fruit on them but they never get to maturity so that we could use them. We've recently discovered that you're supposed to re-pot them every other year so that's what we've done. If we can find a way of giving them more warmth and sunshine and less cold and damp as well as the tender loving care of re-potting and fertiliser, maybe we'll get some fruit.

But actually we quite like having the trees anyway. We don't need them to produce fruit so we're not like the man in the story who did. Every inch of ground in a vineyard needed to be productive because productive ground was scarce. Jesus is very practical. If your fig tree doesn't produce fruit, get rid of it and grow something that will. The vineyard owner's profits and livelihood are being compromised by another season caring for a tree that is unlikely to produce fruit even after that. It has been given every reasonable chance already and another year is beyond the call of duty. The gardener is appealing to a sentimentality that's getting closer to our attitude to our fig trees rather than the hard-nosed business attitude that the owner needs to preserve.

So we're going against Jesus' advice here. We'll keep our fig trees whether or not they produce fruit even after another season's tender loving care.

That's about the extent of Jesus' advice about growing fig trees. He doesn't cater for the gardener who has the luxury of being able to grow trees for their ornamental value rather than for their fruit. But, as we know, when Jesus talked about gardening he was always giving spiritual and theological advice rather than horticultural advice.

So what's he getting at here?

As usual the context of the story helps us understand. In Luke 13:1-5 Jesus has heard news of the Galileans killed by Pilate whose blood was mixed with their sacrifices. Probably what was going on here was that these Galileans were in Jerusalem to offer sacrifices and took the opportunity to protest about Pilate's use of Temple money to pay for the much needed repair and renewal of the water system. Greater than necessary force was probably used by Pilate's police and these Galileans were killed. To add gross offence to the injury he maliciously and vindictively mixed their blood with their sacrifices – 'pour encourager les outres'.

Jesus has simply been told the news but his reaction indicates his insight into the motives of those who told him and he takes the opportunity to teach about God.

"Do you think that these Galileans were worse sinners than all the other Galileans because they suffered this way? I tell you, no!" (NIV)

And to make sure they got the point, Jesus raised another contemporary issue. What do we think about the morality of people who get killed or suffer in natural disaster? Eighteen people had been killed when the Tower of Siloam collapsed on them. Jesus mentioned that and asked, *"Do you think they were more guilty than all the others living in Jerusalem?"* They probably thought those eighteen were guiltier, especially if they were in a position to be killed by that falling tower because they were working on Pilate's water main repairs. But Jesus provided the same answer: *"I tell you, no!"*

We cannot conclude that someone who suffers much, whether through the actions of others or through illness or being caught up in accident or disaster, is any worse a sinner than anyone else. "Those who died when storms and floods swept through northern Britain last winter, were they more guilty that all the others? I tell you, no!"

An individual's suffering is not in proportion to that individual's sin.

That in itself would have been hard for Jesus' listeners to get their minds around. Similarly, today people need to be told because it is an assumption too readily made that our suffering is because of our sin. Many people who are suffering through illness or otherwise ask the question, "What have I done to deserve this?" or even, "I must have been very wicked to suffer this way." There may have been some physical cause but it is not because of sin or wickedness. Suffering is not punishment.

Before we come back to the fig tree we need to notice something else Jesus said in the conversation before he told the story. Each time he had denied the connection between the individual sufferers' sins he said, *"But unless you repent you will all perish."* (NIV)

It is significant that he didn't say, "You need to repent or you'll perish, and so do you, and you, and you." He's not addressing individuals; he's deliberately referring to them all collectively.

This is not so much a spiritual message in the guise of horticulture as a political message in the guise of theology. The actions and attitudes of Jesus' Jewish questioners reflected in this conversation are of a desire to build a Jewish kingdom over and against the Roman rule. Effectively Jesus says, "Unless you turn from the ways of the world, unless you stop trying to build your own worldly kingdom of power and status based upon an overinflated view of your own importance, the nation will be crushed by the power and might of Rome."

There's no clairvoyance, no crystal ball involved in that prediction. It's political realism which proved right in AD70 with the fall of Jerusalem.

But it's not just political realism. Jesus is also saying that a nation that is given great responsibility, and that received better than the average chance to lead people in God's ways and knowledge of God, will be judged according to that responsibility and the gifts it is given.

Jesus told the parable to help us understand that God treats individuals differently from nations.

Jesus is saying that a nation that has great gifts and a key place in God's scheme, a nation that has great responsibility to lead the world in the ways of peace and justice, freedom and mercy, will be judged and answerable for the way those responsibilities and gifts were used.

Nations, organisations and communities that don't match up, that don't bear fruit, will be cut down. Those nations, organisations and communities – including churches – that are given every chance but don't use their chances and gifts to lead others and influence the world for God's ways will suffer the results unless they turn their ways around and live up to their calling.

There are also hard questions for individuals arising from this parable. The fig tree was useless; it was using up the soil. The fig tree took out of the economy of the vineyard more than it put in. Do we take out of God's world more than we put in or do we work to put in at least as much as we take out? Are we useless or do we produce fruit according to the gifts and nurture we receive?

The encouraging news from the parable is that God is merciful. It is not all hardnosed economics. We don't have to be able to show a positive balance sheet or a year-on-year increase in our fruit production in order not to be cut out. God is a God of second chances. There are many witnesses to that through the Bible and through Christian history. Many of us would no longer be planted in God's vineyard being nurtured, dug around and fertilised if we'd been cut out as soon as we didn't produce fruit.

God is a God of second chances, even third, fourth, fifth chances, and so on.

But... You knew there was a 'but' coming, didn't you? But the hard message of this parable comes at the end. God is a God of second chances but he is also a God who gives a last chance. The gardener was given permission to dig around the fig tree and fertilise it for one more season. If it didn't produce fruit, then it would be cut down.

It is not that God finally gets impatient – like the Roman authorities. It is more that God makes appeal after appeal to us to come into his kingdom, gives us opportunity after opportunity to follow in his ways. Eventually we could find we have refused so many chances, closed our ears to so many appeals, found a way round so many challenges, missed so many opportunities that we have refused to come in and shut ourselves out from God.

So make every effort to be fruitful by demonstrating his love and mercy, his patience and care, using all the chances you have, all the gifts and opportunities. Seek his ways in all you do. And do all you can to influence in his ways the corporate life of the households, communities and nation of which you are a part.

15

Jesus on the Workforce (iv)

Tenant Farmers

Matthew 21:33-46; Mark 12:1-12; Luke 20:9-19

"Listen to another parable: there was a landowner who planted a vineyard. He put a wall round it, dug a winepress in it and built a watchtower. Then he rented the vineyard to some farmers and moved to another place. When the harvest time approached, he sent his servants to the tenants to collect his fruit. The tenants seized his servants; they beat one, killed another, and stoned a third. Then he sent other servants to them, more than the first time, and the tenants treated them in the same way. Last of all he sent his son to them. 'They will respect my son,' he said. But when the tenants saw the son, they said to each other, 'This is the heir. Come, let's kill him and take his inheritance.' So they took him and threw him out of the vineyard and killed him. Therefore, when the owner of the vineyard comes, what will he do to those tenants?" "He will bring those wretches to a wretched end," they replied, "and he will rent the vineyard to other tenants, who will give him his share of the crop at harvest time." Jesus said to them, "Have you never read in the Scripture: 'The stone the builders rejected has become the cornerstone; the Lord has done this,

and it is marvelous in our eyes'? Therefore I tell you that the kingdom of God will be taken away from you and given to people who will produce its fruit. Anyone who falls on this stone will be broken to pieces, but anyone on whom it falls will be crushed." When the chief priests and the Pharisees heard Jesus' parables, they knew he was talking about them. They looked for a way to arrest him, but they were afraid of the crowd because the people held that he was a prophet.

We don't own a farm, much less a vineyard, but we do own a flat that we rent to three students. There are all sorts of laws and regulations governing rental property that are designed to protect tenants but it is still the case that if the right procedure has been followed, tenants can be evicted if they don't pay the agreed rent. I've been listening to Radio 4's 'The Archers' for long enough to remember when the Grundys were evicted from Grange Farm because they couldn't pay the rent. They had also been unable to fulfil some other conditions of the tenancy such as the upkeep of buildings.

Clearly Jesus is living in a different time and a different culture but the principle is the same. Tenants have to pay rent to the landlord; in this case the owner of the vineyard. This story might be told today as allotment holders renting from the Local Authority. The difference is that the rent is payable in fruit from the harvest. So rather than a monthly or quarterly rent, these tenants have to contribute a proportion of the annual crop. It would be like allotment holders paying the council in potatoes and beans rather than a monthly fee. The way Jesus tells the story it looks as though the servants he sent to collect the contribution would have taken away a certain amount of grapes. Matthew and Mark record that the owner prepared a winepress in the vineyard so rent may have been payable in wine.

It sounds as though this landlord is particularly patient and will ask more than once for the rent that's due. Usually it is the tenant's responsibility to pay the rent that is due rather than the landlord's responsibility to come and collect it but this landlord sends servants – council officers? – to collect the produce that is due.

So far so straightforward, but it would hardly be a story worth telling if it simply ended that they paid up in so many cases of the best Cabernet Sauvignon. The story gets interesting because the tenants decide not to pay the rent. Matthew, Mark and Luke all have slightly different versions of what the tenants did to which of the servants but the summary is probably good enough for us. They treated them shamefully, beat them up, killed or stoned them. If tenants or allotment holders were to treat rent collectors in the way the evangelists describe, they would quickly be arrested on a charge of assault and probably grievous bodily harm, if not murder. This landlord again surprises us with his patience but also perhaps with his naivety. He's seen the way his servants were treated but still he doesn't send in the bailiffs with eviction notices. He sends his son thinking they would respect him. It's like the Chief Executive of the council sending his deputy to collect the rent thinking that pulling rank will make a difference.

To modern ears this is where the story starts to stretch our sense of credibility. If a property owner dies without an heir, it doesn't mean that his tenants inherit, so why did those tenants think they would inherit if they killed the heir to the vineyard? There must be some different property and inheritance law applicable here. It is possible that in Jesus' time the tenants would have been in line to inherit. Certainly, about twenty centuries before Jesus, Abraham faced the possibility of dying childless and a servant in his household was to be his heir (Genesis 15:1-4).

So, maybe the tenants would have inherited if the owner had died without an heir. But they reckoned without the power of the landlord. Due process of law seems to have been very different in Jesus' day. There are no eviction notices, no solicitor's letters, no court summonses. In all versions of the story Jesus asks the question, *"What will the owner of the vineyard do?"* Mark and Luke record this as a rhetorical question to which Jesus supplies the answer, *"He will come and kill those tenants and give the vineyard to others."*[21] Interestingly, Matthew records Jesus' hearers as giving an answer: *"He will bring those wretches to a wretched end, and he will rent the vineyard to other tenants who will give him his share of the crop at harvest time."*[22]

---

[21] Mark 12:9; Luke 20:16
[22] Matthew 21:41

All of those reactions might now be regarded as a bit harsh. The tenants might have been on a murder charge, but the law doesn't permit this kind of vigilante justice. Due process of law requires prosecution and all reasonable steps to be taken to recover the rent that is due. Contracts cannot be drawn up to say that if rent collectors are badly treated the landlord can come in and beat up the tenants.

As usual Jesus is not talking about gardening or farming or landlord-tenant relationships. There are three major clues to what is going on behind the text of this parable. Firstly, Jesus sets the story in a vineyard, not a farm or an allotment or a student flat. Secondly, the last messenger that is sent to collect the rent is the owner's son. Thirdly, Jesus' comments, as recorded with slight variations by all three evangelists, make the connections fairly explicit.

The story is set in a vineyard. Luke edits the introductory section probably because he's writing for a non-Jewish audience. Matthew, writing for a Jewish audience, preserves what is probably the earlier written form of the story from Mark:

"A man planted a vineyard. He put a wall round it, dug a pit for the winepress and built a watchtower."

Jewish audiences and Christians since, with knowledge of the Jewish Scriptures in the Old Testament, will see the connection. The vineyard has been a motif for Israel. When Jesus talks about a vineyard he's talking about the people of Israel.

God's people are meant to provide fruit for God out of their lives lived in his service. It is clear to Christians reading this that Jesus was referring to himself as the last messenger sent to collect the rent. Jesus coming as God's Son is the one who will inherit, the one who will rule in God's kingdom and he is sent to bring in the harvest, the fruit of the vineyard, as other messengers, the prophets, have been rejected.

Both Mark and Luke's accounts of this parable immediately follow Jesus' debate with chief priests, teachers of the law and elders about recognition of authority. Matthew inserts the Parable of the Two Sons at harvest time in the vineyard in between.[23] When challenged about his own authority Jesus had asked a question about

---

[23] see chapter 13

John the Baptist to see to what extent they recognized the authority behind a messenger. The conclusion we draw from that exchange is that they do understand the authority of God behind John the Baptist and therefore also behind Jesus but they won't acknowledge it because it doesn't fit with their view of their own position.

Jesus tells this story to show the results of their policy. Matthew's version has the chief priests and elders pronounce the verdict on themselves, Mark and Luke only record Jesus pronouncing judgment on them.

Once we've understood that the story is about Israel and God's relationship with them through Jesus we can see that Jesus' comments afterwards fall into place. Jesus changes the metaphor by referring to Psalm 118:22-23. The rent collector has become a stone at first rejected by those entrusted with building but which has been recognized by others for its importance and is now the cornerstone, the most important in the building.

Finally, the point is spelt out as the parallel slips in Jesus' summary from Matthew 21:43:

"Therefore I tell you that the kingdom of God will be taken away from you and given to a people who will produce its fruit."

Obviously, as all three evangelists record, the Jewish authorities listening could tell that he had told the parable against them. It was not about paying rent on time. It was about recognizing what is due to God and who his messengers are. It was about keeping a proper humility about our own position in relation to God who does not owe us a place in his kingdom. Rather, we owe to him the fruit of our labour in his vineyard.

16

Jesus on Viticulture

How to Bear Fruit

John 15:1-6

[Jesus said], "I am the true vine and my Father is the gardener. He cuts off every branch in me that bears no fruit, while every branch that does bear fruit he prunes so that it will be even more fruitful. You are already clean because of the word I have spoken to you. Remain in me, as I also remain in you. No branch can bear fruit by itself; it must remain in the vine. Neither can you bear fruit unless you remain in me. I am the vine; you are the branches. If you remain in me and I in you, you will bear much fruit; apart from me you can do nothing. If you do not remain in me, you are like a branch that is thrown away and withers; such branches are picked up, thrown into the fire and burned."

This is one of Jesus' most detailed pieces of gardening advice. From these verses we learn that branches of a vine that do not bear fruit need to be cut away from the vine. Moreover, once removed Jesus indicates that they are good for nothing but to be thrown out. He also shows us that careful pruning is important even of branches that do bear fruit. Once the grapes have been picked from a vine, not only are fruitless branches removed but the fruitful ones are pruned back so as to produce more fruit next year. Finally, Jesus teaches us that a branch separate from the vine won't bear fruit.

A visit to a vineyard, or a quick search through a gardening book or online, will confirm that all this is correct procedure for growing vines. The only additional information likely to be needed is to do with soil, aspect and climate. Good drainage, south-facing aspect and warm sunshine for ripening will all help. Clearly Jesus majors on the care of the vine once you've got it in the ground.

In many ways Jesus is the master at getting a point across in as succinct a way as possible but even for him six verses on care for vines is a bit brief and he really only spends one verse on viticulture; the rest is making a spiritual and theological point out of the gardening advice.

As usual Jesus is less concerned about the quality of the grapes we grow in our gardens and more concerned with the spiritual fruit of our connection with him.

He chooses the growing of vines as his illustration for a reason. There is a rich vein of vineyard theology in the Old Testament and his hearers would have been familiar with it.

The immediate physical context of this saying is a little ambiguous. At the end of chapter 14 Jesus invited his disciples to go with him out of the Upper Room where they had shared the Last Supper and where he had spoken with them about betrayal and denial, about love for one another and the coming of the Holy Spirit, the Comforter, Helper or Advocate.

Original and early manuscripts would not have had chapter divisions or headings so *"Come now; let us leave"* follows directly on to *"I am the true vine…"* Did they not leave after all; did Jesus continue talking until the beginning of chapter 18 when we're told, *"When he had finished praying, Jesus left with his disciples…"*? Or did they leave the Upper Room between chapters 14 and 15? That would mean that chapters 15 to 17 were spoken outside. Maybe they stopped somewhere – perhaps near to the Temple – where Jesus prayed with and for them. They could then have left that place and left the city at the beginning of chapter 18 to go to the Garden of Gethsemane on the other side of the Kidron Valley.

When the Bible is unclear it leaves room for imagination and conjecture. As long as we don't build too much of our faith on aspects of this it can help us a good deal. I like to think that the context for this saying was as they passed the Temple with the Golden Vine on the porch. In the Upper Room Jesus had been speaking of the Cup of Blessing, saying that it was his blood of the new covenant and that he would not drink of the fruit of the vine until the kingdom of God would come. This must have been puzzling to them to say the least. Perhaps passing the Golden Vine on the Temple porch gave Jesus an opportunity for an explanation; an explanation dressed up in the form of gardening advice.

In much of the vineyard theology of the Old Testament the nation of Israel is depicted as the vine and God is the keeper of the vineyard. Jesus picks up these aspects in other places when he talks about the workforce and who has care of the vines. Here he wants them to think about care of the vine and about wine production because he has been talking about wine and about his body and blood.

So often in the Old Testament the vine as an image for Israel was used to show their failure. The true vine stands for what Israel was called to be. Jesus is telling them that God's purpose in Israel is being fulfilled in him. In his person he sums up and gathers together the whole people of God. In that way his disciples and followers – we, his church, the contemporary people of God – are a part of him, are incorporated into him.

The image Jesus uses is very carefully put together. He doesn't say that he is the stem of the vine and we are the branches. He says that he is the vine – the whole vine – and we are the branches. Branches are parts of the vine; we are parts of him.

It is only as part of the vine that any branch can bear fruit because it is as part of the vine, connected to the vine, that the life of the vine flows through it. Here the metaphors become mixed as we see Jesus' thought processes swinging easily backwards and forwards between the image of the vine with its production of grapes and wine and the image of wine being drunk as the blood of the covenant.

John sets his account of Jesus talking of eating the flesh and drinking the blood of the Son of Man back in chapter 6 after feeding the five thousand. Jewish food laws forbid the eating of meat with the blood in it. Eating meat would for many have been a luxury and a special occasion. Eating meat that had been part of a sacrifice in the Temple – the neatest equivalent to a restaurant – might have been a once-in-a-lifetime occasion. To eat the flesh of the sacrifice stood for taking in and identifying as one's own the spiritual power of the sacrifice. So, to eat the flesh of the Son of Man is to receive the power of Jesus' self-giving sacrifice. Flesh from which the blood is removed is dead. To eat Jesus' flesh in the bread of communion is to identify with Jesus' death, to become a part of that death and make it our own.

It was expressly forbidden in the Jewish food laws to eat the flesh with the life blood still in it. To be told they had to drink his blood would have been difficult to understand at best and anathema at worst. Pouring out the blood of the sacrifice is, by way of death, releasing the life to God. So to drink the blood of the Son of Man through the wine of communion is to identify with Jesus' risen life, become part of that life and make it our own.

Only when connected to the vine do we have the life of the vine flowing through us to produce the fruit of the vine. As Jesus said in his comments on his flesh and blood in John chapter 6, those gifts are real food and drink and those who receive them and make them their own live in him and he in them. As he says here, *"Remain in me as I also remain in you."*

So we reach the "yes but how" moment when you want to say, "Yes, I just about follow that complicated path through several mixed metaphors, but how do we remain in him, how do we remain connected to the vine? What does that mean in practical terms?"

Again it is linked to what we know about how vines produce fruit.

"No branch can bear fruit by itself; it must remain in the vine. Neither can you bear fruit unless you remain in me."[24]

OK, so that's the imperative stated again; we get the message, we are to remain in him or we won't bear fruit. But still we want to ask, "How do we remain in him?"

Jesus goes on putting apparently the same things slightly differently and perhaps here we get a clue as to the 'how'.

---

[24] verse 4

"I am the vine; you are the branches. If you remain in me and I in you, you will bear much fruit; apart from me you can do nothing."

It seems the whole essence of Christian life and discipleship is this mutual indwelling: we in him and he in us. It is not so much how we achieve this as how we know it to be the case. Jesus has already said that no one comes to him unless the Father draws them and that the way to the Father is through him. All forms of Christian worship and discipline have this mutual indwelling as their object. So communion in particular and worship in general, prayer, Bible reading and study, through which we come to know God better and align ourselves and our desires ever more closely to his, are ways in which we 'remain in him'. The more we learn to align ourselves with the ways and values, the desires and longings of the kingdom and the more we pray 'in his name', the more we remain in him.

It is slightly frustrating for those of us who like a how-to manual that Jesus doesn't give us a step by step guide to being and remaining in him. He doesn't do that because obedience to him and being in him are not a matter of law – doing certain things – but a matter of love and trust. As John put it elsewhere,[25] *"This is his command: to believe in the name of his Son, Jesus Christ, and to love one another as he commanded us."*

What he does give us is a succinct guide to knowing that we are in him, a branch connected to the vine, rather than one of those branches that has been separated from the vine and is now good for nothing but being burnt. Jesus' reference to branches that do not bear fruit and are useless also picks up a well known and recognisable piece of Old Testament vineyard theology.

"How is the wood of a vine different from that of a branch from any of the trees in the forest? Is wood ever taken from it to make anything useful? Do they make pegs from it to hang things on? And after it is thrown on the fire as fuel and the fire burns both ends and chars the middle, is it then useful for anything?"[26]

---

[25] 1 John 3:23 (NIV)
[26] Ezekiel 14:2-4 (NIV)

The implied answer to all Ezekiel's questions is no. Separate from the vine, its wood is useless except as firewood. On the other hand, as Jesus says, *"I am the vine, you are the branches. If you remain in me and I in you, you will bear much fruit."*

It is not a case of doing something to be in him and sitting back and enjoying the fruit. There is Christian worship and discipline to engage with through prayer, Bible reading and study; the spiritual disciplines of fasting, silence, solitude and sacrifice; worship, service, celebration and fellowship. All of this helps us to draw close, to follow in his paths as the Father draws us. And then there are opportunities to be taken which, with his life running through us, will produce fruit for the kingdom.

It's difficult to speak of fruit in these terms without thinking of what St Paul called the fruit of the Spirit in Galatians 5:22-23: love, joy, peace, patience, kindness, goodness, faithfulness, gentleness, and self-control. It is not an exhaustive list of what Jesus might have meant by fruit but it is a good enough starting point for our purposes. A life lived in connection with the vine, with the life of the vine flowing through us, with the life blood of Jesus in our veins, will, through the caring, service and outreach we undertake as we have opportunity, produce fruit in love, joy, peace, patience, kindness, goodness, faithfulness, gentleness, and self-control.

So, do our prayers and do our actions produce fruit? Do we grow in grace? Do we desire his will rather than our own? Does the world become just a bit more peaceful and kind through our words and actions; do we see more love and gentleness; as we grow in faithfulness and self-control do we see more patience and goodness around us?

Challenging questions, but these are the characteristics that a wine taster is looking for from the fruit of this particular vine.

17

Nearer to God in a Garden?

Maundy Thursday Evening in Gethsemane

Matthew 26:36-46; Mark 14:32-42; Luke 22:39-46

And in the garden secretly,
and on the cross on high,
should teach his followers,
and inspire to suffer and to die.

John Henry Newman[27]

They went to a place called Gethsemane, and Jesus said to his
disciples, "Sit here while I pray." He took Peter, James and
John along with him, and he began to be deeply distressed and
troubled. "My soul is overwhelmed with sorrow to the point
of death," he said to them. "Stay here and keep watch."
Going a little farther, he fell to the ground and prayed that if
possible the hour might pass from him. "Abba, Father," he
said, "everything is possible for you. Take this cup from me.
Yet not what I will, but what you will." Then he returned to

---

[27] 'Praise to the holiest in the height', John Henry Newman (1801-1890);
verse 6; adapted by Compilers of Hymns for Today's Church 1982 (alt.)
Reproduced from Singing the Faith Electronic Words Edition, number 334

his disciples and found them sleeping. "Simon," he said to Peter, "are you asleep? Couldn't you keep watch for one hour? Watch and pray so that you will not fall into temptation. The spirit is willing, but the flesh is weak." Once more he went away and prayed the same thing. When he came back, he again found them sleeping, because their eyes were heavy. They did not know what to say to him.

Returning the third time, he said to them, "Are you still sleeping and resting? Enough! The hour has come. Look, the Son of Man is delivered into the hands of sinners. Rise! Let us go! Here comes my betrayer!"

Many people find coming to church – literally coming into the church building – a difficult thing to do. Unlike other places where people are to be enticed in – like shops in shopping centres – churches make it difficult. We have great big solid doors with handles that you need weight training to lift and interiors that are hard to see even if the door is open. You don't know what you're letting yourself in for from outside; you can't see who, if anyone, is already there or what they're doing. The kinds of anxieties raised in a potential but cautious worshipper's mind are likely to get in the way of any anticipation of the presence of God if they should pluck up the courage to enter.

It is not just the physical nature of the entrances to our buildings that works against people's coming to God. The cultural shift in people's minds and approach and their lack of familiarity with religious things and ways means that they describe themselves as "spiritual but not religious" because their perception of traditional religion has become an alien and off-putting experience. By no means all, but many of the "spiritual but not religious" find their experience of the Transcendent, the Other or the Spiritual among 'nature' – countryside; hills, mountains; plants; an expanse of sky whether clear, bright and blue or dark and menacing or dark, clear and starry. Some would say that a stroll in a park or a garden where plants have been carefully selected, placed and planted with a mass of colour against a backdrop of trees and shrubs that can be viewed from well laid out paths and strategically placed, secluded benches gives a greater sense of connection with something outside of themselves and their own mundane human existence than churches, however majestic the music, however compelling the preaching and however warm the welcome.

Many people would say that they are nearer to God in a garden.

One church where I minister has noticed and addressed the problem of the distance people are from the church in their daily lives and concerns from entering a church for worship. We think of what we do across the life and activities of the church community as stepping stones for people towards a relationship with God and his people. These stepping stones include a coffee morning each week, an annual 'Big Lunch' in the church car park (under the trees), a monthly 'Big Breakfast' service, a food bank where regulars come and share coffee and cake and take home a parcel of food to tie them over when the money doesn't make it to the end of the week. All these help to bring people a little bit closer.

The area in front of the church has been a bit neglected, with gates shut and the space kept under control but never developed. It is people from among the food bank users who decided to turn this area into a garden. With some funding from the church, a policy to leave the gates open, some plants, pots and a good deal of voluntary time it has become a community garden in front of the church. It makes the whole site welcoming and attractive, and people come and spend a few minutes (or possibly hours) sitting in quiet contemplation or conversation.

I expect they do other things as well but this garden has become another stepping stone – not one we set out to put in place but one laid by those we would like to see crossing them. It meant that the obvious location for the annual Open Air service in the summer was the garden at the front rather than the car park at the back. It was also clear that it should include a dedication of the garden. Open Air services as a stepping stone have been part of the programme for some time but this attracted people from the food bank and people who'd come to the Big Lunch as well as church members and friends.

Suddenly, people were in church without crossing a threshold. The edges have been blurred and the anxieties have been bypassed. The worship, the singing, the prayers and the message combined with well chosen responses for the dedication of the garden that made parallels between aspects of the garden such as its soil, plants, flowers, produce and so on and our relationships with God and his people meant that people felt closer to God in a garden.

The garden is not a formal religious place but it is somewhere that personal and corporate spiritual things can happen.

Now I'm not suggesting that Maundy Thursday evening services ought to take place outdoors in whatever churchyard, garden or car park there may be around the church. Thursday evenings in March and April in this country can be dark, cold and damp – not to mention soaking wet. That is not often a very spiritual experience and not to be encouraged on what is one of the most significant and poignant moments in the Christian calendar.

There are so many themes for Maundy Thursday that it is not possible to cover them all every year. We commemorate the Last Supper and share bread and wine in order to know that he is still among us and that his death and resurrection are for us and include us.

Hearing the account of Jesus washing his disciples' feet, we also remember that we are called to a life of love and service to our Lord.

Recalling that Judas left the supper and went out into the night to 'do what he had to do' – to betray Jesus, leading Temple guards to him with swords and clubs to arrest him – we look deep into ourselves and acknowledge the ways in which we betray him, desert him and let him down.

Just as Peter three times denied that he even knew Jesus and all the others ran away, we may not think of ourselves in the same bracket as Judas but we know that we'd have been with them – probably not even brave enough to follow at a distance but certainly with a priority for self-preservation.

In between all that it is easy to forget that the supper was a formal religious event. This was a Passover supper or something very like it. At the end of supper they sang a hymn. Jesus had prayed and spoken words that invested that occasion with greater and different significance than they had heard before but it was a formal religious occasion. Yet Jesus knew what was coming and he knew that religion wasn't all that was needed. We are concerned that people have stepping stones into relationship with God and his people but it seems that Jesus was aware that we also need stepping stones between formal (or informal) corporate religious worship and a deep, meaningful personal relationship with God with or without the presence of others from his people.

Maundy Thursday evening seems to show that it is possible to be nearer to God in a garden.

Amongst the olive groves on the sparse soil and short, stunted plants, Jesus went a distance from most of his disciples, taking his closest friends with him but then leaving them a short distance away. He sought the seclusion of a space in the garden to pray; to come close to God and face what he knew was coming.

He began to be sorrowful and troubled. Luke's description of his sweat as like great drops of blood indicates human stress and anxiety levels beyond anything most of us can imagine. Mark's record that Jesus used the address *"Abba"* indicates the closeness of his relationship with God. 'Abba', usually translated 'Father' is more like 'Daddy' or 'Papa' – the familiar, close, intimate address of a child who knows himself in a mutual relationship of love and trust.

This is the moment, in the garden, when Jesus comes closest to God in our Gospel accounts. Three times in his anguish and fear he brings to God his prayer that he might not have to go through the pain, the humiliation, the death and separation that he sees ahead. And three times he expresses his trust in his heavenly Father by saying, *"Not as I will, but as you will,"* *"May your will be done."*

> *In the garden secretly*
> *And on the cross on high ...*
> *To suffer and to die.*[28]

So let's take challenge and encouragement both from Jesus' closeness to God in the Garden of Gethsemane and from the disciples who were also in that garden. They couldn't do what was asked of them. Instead of staying awake and keeping watch, they fell asleep. They were exhausted by the events of the past few days; they were perplexed by the words and actions of Jesus that evening; they were afraid of what may be to come; they could go on no longer. After some chiding and prodding into action Jesus realised their needs – he does not push us beyond endurance but he does expect us to push ourselves to our limits. And we can be encouraged that we are to

---

[28] Ibid.

participate with him in a 'both-and' relationship with God. It is both a public, corporate relationship and a private, intimate relationship.

In the garden secretly and on the cross on high.

As we shall hear tomorrow it was on the cross that Jesus found God to be the more distant. *"My God, why have you forsaken me?"* from the cross contrasts with the intimate and trusting *"not what I will but what you will be done"* in the garden.

Sometimes the stepping stones we lay for others to come closer to God turn out to be stepping stones for us who are already in a public relationship to come to a closer personal, private, intimate relationship. As we go with Jesus to Gethsemane may we also know that we too can be nearer to God in a garden.

18

Burial Garden (i)

Good Friday[29]

John 19:38-42

Later, Joseph of Arimathea asked Pilate for the body of Jesus. Now Joseph was a disciple of Jesus, but secretly because he feared the Jewish leaders. With Pilate's permission, he came and took the body away. He was accompanied by Nicodemus, the man who earlier had visited Jesus at night. Nicodemus brought a mixture of myrrh and aloes, about thirty-five kilograms. Taking Jesus' body, the two of them wrapped it, with the spices, in strips of linen. This was in accordance with Jewish burial customs. At the place where Jesus was crucified, there was a garden, and in the garden a new tomb, in which no-one had ever been laid. Because it was the Jewish day of Preparation and since the tomb was near by, they laid Jesus there.

Many churchyards and cemeteries are beautiful places. Indeed, many are called a Garden of Rest or Garden of Remembrance. What

---

[29] A final reflection for Good Friday which might come towards the end of a service at the Cross.

John describes as the place of Jesus' burial was probably a sizeable private garden, an orchard or plantation.

The image is not of a public cemetery kept like a park. It is likely that it belonged to Joseph of Arimathea or Nicodemus, who took charge of the arrangements, or to one of their friends. These are clearly wealthy and influential figures. Joseph has enough influence with Pilate to be allowed to take Jesus' body in spite of the Governor's difficulties and sensitivities surrounding Jesus' reputation, the charges on which he was executed and the Jewish Council's views. Nicodemus was a member of the Council, and John recorded and refers here to his nocturnal visit to Jesus.[30] Both of them were rich, powerful and influential and both of them were followers of Jesus but secretly, timidly or cautiously. But something made them change, come out of the shadows and quite publicly do the right thing.

What John describes is the 'right thing' in several ways. They did the right things by the Jewish laws and customs. They ensured a burial before the Passover Sabbath began. They took the right spices and they wrapped Jesus' body using linen cloths with spices between the layers. The linen cloths are reminiscent of John's description of Lazarus's grave cloths. The spices alone indicate something of Joseph of Arimathea's wealth: 100lbs weight or about 35kg is an enormous amount. The whole description adds up to a burial that could be described as lavish but for the fact that it was hurried and also clearly meant to be temporary.

This garden tomb was not intended to be Jesus' last resting place. Many tombs would be used more than once, and perhaps contain several bodies at a time, but be only a temporary resting place until a permanent tomb was found or constructed. In accordance with the customs Jesus' body would have been laid in a tomb that was nearby and handy for family and friends to mourn and remember. This may have been for a period of days or longer. It may be that it was only intended to be until the Sabbath was over or it may have been for a year when a permanent place of burial would be found. When they buried him they didn't know how temporary a resting place it would be.

---

[30] John 3:1-21

The tomb had not yet been used so it was not made 'unclean' by contact with the dead and there could be no confusion about which body was which.

That tells us quite a bit about what happened. So, what's going on? John seldom includes details without there being a secondary meaning beyond the factual.

Jesus was buried in accordance with the Sabbath law which had so often been the point of controversy and the reason for conspiracy to have him killed. Perhaps this indicates the triumph of the old system. Perhaps the hurried burial completed just as night was falling also indicates the triumph of the powers of darkness. Light and darkness are powerful and recurrent themes in John's Gospel from the prologue through to Judas's exit from the supper when *"it was night"* and the coming to Gethsemane to arrest him in the darkness.

Maybe John shows that the old system and the power of darkness have triumphed.

But John also points out that this took place in a garden.

Maybe we can see another connection here indicating that this triumph is as temporary as the place of burial.

Maybe John is giving a hint that points towards what is to follow and what might be going on. This is not the triumph of the old system or the triumph of the power of darkness. Maybe this garden hints at a return to another garden. Maybe this is the beginning of the return to the intended relationships before there was a system and before darkness crept in to have power over people. The Garden of Eden was the garden, literally, of 'delight'. This burial garden pointed out as a temporary resting place was to become the Garden of Delight – the garden of light, the garden of life, the garden of resurrection – the garden from which all new life, all eternal life will flow. But that is a story for another day, a thought that will have to wait for Sunday.

19

Burial Garden (ii)

Easter Day

John 20:1-18

Early on the first day of the week, while it was still dark, Mary Magdalene went to the tomb and saw that the stone had been removed from the entrance. So she came running to Simon Peter and the other disciple, the one Jesus loved, and said, "They have taken the Lord out of the tomb, and we don't know where they have put him!" So Peter and the other disciple started for the tomb. Both were running, but the other disciple outran Peter and reached the tomb first. He bent over and looked in at the strips of linen lying there but did not go in. Then Simon Peter came along behind him and went straight into the tomb. He saw the strips of linen lying there, as well as the cloth that had been wrapped round Jesus' head. The cloth was still lying in its place, separate from the linen. Finally, the other disciple, who had reached the tomb first, also went inside. He saw and believed. (They still did not understand from Scripture that Jesus had to rise from the dead.) Then the disciples went back to where they were staying. Now Mary stood outside the tomb crying. As she wept, she bent over to look into the tomb and saw two angels in white, seated where Jesus' body had been, one at the head and the other at the foot. They asked her, "Woman, why are you crying?" "They have taken my Lord away," she said, "and I don't know where they have put him." At this, she turned round and saw Jesus standing there, but she did not realise that it was Jesus. He asked her, "Woman, why are you crying? Who is it you are looking for?" Thinking he was the gardener, she said, "Sir, if you have carried him away, tell me where you have put him, and I will get him." Jesus said to her, "Mary." She turned towards him and cried out in Aramaic, "Rabboni!" (which means "Teacher"). Jesus said, "Do not hold on to me, for I have not yet ascended to the Father. Go instead to my brothers and tell them, 'I am ascending to my Father and your Father, to my God and your God.'" Mary Magdalene went to the disciples with the news: "I have seen the Lord!" And she told them that he had said these things to her.

We need to go back for a moment to Friday evening.

Mary's world has fallen apart.

Jesus had been instrumental in her healing. Whatever it meant to have seven demons, it was a condition that covered the whole range of mental disorder with physical and social symptoms and consequences. She had followed him, listened to him, learnt from him and devoted herself, her time and her resources to him.

He died about three o'clock on Friday afternoon and by the time they'd buried him all she could do was wait through Saturday – probably the longest Sabbath of her life – until it was just getting light on Sunday morning.

At the earliest possible moment (perhaps a bit before if truth be told) she set out to do the only practical things left to do – take spices to do for Jesus' body what she had no time for on Friday. Maybe she went with others, maybe alone, probably for those practical purposes but also just to be in the place where they'd laid him in such a hurry.

Fundamentally what Mary was doing was simply about grief. Part of mourning is the desire for the person who has died, a yearning to be with them; perhaps an awareness of things never said, or things that would have been better left unsaid, maybe questions never asked about things never understood.

We know that being nearer to where the body lies makes no real practical difference but it is where we want to be because it helps us feel a closeness, which is what we are missing.

Early on the first day of the week, while it was still dark, Mary Magdalene went to the tomb and saw that the stone had been removed from the entrance. She went and told Peter and John who came and checked it out – a woman's testimony didn't count. John saw and believed. Well, he believed what she'd told him: the stone had been rolled away and his body wasn't there. Peter and John went back to the room where she'd found them probably puzzled and nervous. Surely if Joseph of Arimathea and Nicodemus had already been to move Jesus to a more permanent burial site they would have told them.

But Mary stayed outside the tomb crying.

Her world has not yet begun to make sense in her grief and bereavement but now it has had another blow. She can't even do the practical thing she came for. All that is left is grief and the painful hole in her life where Jesus has been – a large painful hole since she has filled her life with his presence, devoted herself to his needs, hung on his every word, and relied on him for her self-esteem, her self-knowledge and her place in a community.

At this stage, with everything so raw, with the shock of Friday still fresh and the new shock of his body being missing leaving her numb and confused, all she can do is weep. She stays outside the tomb crying.

And, as you do, because always when something is missing you go back to the place you last saw it, you check again the place where it should be – whether it's the car keys or the body of a loved one – she bends down and looks into the tomb.

Am I imagining things? Am I having a nightmare? Was it still dark and I was crying so much I missed something?

She checks; she bends down to look.

And then, another shock – two angels in white. They weren't there a moment ago when Peter and John went in; where did they come from? Who are they? What do they want?

It is all very confusing.

Two strange-looking angelic visitors to an unoccupied tomb. Then someone else she doesn't recognise; surely the gardener, no one else would be in the garden so early. Maybe the gardener had a reason to move this particular body.

In all the confusion, maybe the morning mist and the half-darkness and her tears, she doesn't recognise him.

It's the use of her name that does it. We'll never know how he said it, what was the tone of voice he used. No doubt you've heard people use your name in many different ways.

Was there some reproach in this tone because she didn't recognise him? Was it a soft tone of endearment? Was he slightly cross that she hadn't understood enough to realise this was what would happen? Was he just attracting her attention in the way he often had when he wanted to tell her something? Was it in a tone that pointed out who he was – a kind of "hey, it's me" sort of "Mary"?

You may be able to think of many more possibilities.

Whatever it was, it was enough and Mary's world did another somersault – the second time that day and the third time in as many days. If he was here, as alive as she was, then he wasn't dead. Was it too much to hope that even if the whole coming-of-the-kingdom thing that he'd talked about didn't happen, perhaps they could get back to normal, maybe go back to Galilee, back to the days of popularity, of teaching, listening to his stories, watching the signs and wonders as he brought joy, hope and laughter along with his challenges?

Probably it *was* too much. She was running ahead of herself. For now, it was enough that he was here. She wanted to hold him, to know the reality of that solid presence, to cry into his shoulder out of relief and confusion.

But again he speaks and again her world turns:

"Do not hold on to me, because I have not yet ascended to the Father. But go to my brothers and say to them, 'I am ascending to my Father and your Father, to my God and your God.'"

What was that all about? Holding on to him is all she wants to do at the moment but it's the one thing he tells her not to do. And what's all this about ascending to the Father; and moreover, is he telling her to do something? Again, a woman on her own with a message of what she's seen, a message for his brothers – the other followers? She just wants some time with him, but he's telling her to let go, not to come *with* him but to go *from* him; not 'come and see' this time, as he has said to many before, but 'go and tell'.

But that's exactly it. The resurrection turned Mary's world upside down; the resurrection changed everything. We get the story, we've heard it before, we know and we have some understanding in our heads about the dawning of hope, the triumph of love, the ultimate eternal truth that contrary to popular opinion and general appearance it is not death that has the last word but life.

We get that but we get too used to that.

Jesus is saying to Mary that's she's got to get a bigger understanding of what he's all about, a broader view of what's going on. She can't cling to the old ways, she can't hold on to the relationship that she had where she knew she was safe in his presence, where she could reach out and touch him, speak to him and ask whatever she wanted, hear what he had to say, all close and personal and located in Galilee – or perhaps Jerusalem.

Jesus is saying that it is all bigger than that. He's ascending to the Father. It's not going back to how it was; it's moving forward into a completely new dimension. He tried to explain this at the supper on Thursday. The accounts indicate that Mary wasn't there so she wouldn't remember let alone understand, but later it would become clear in practical terms that he went so his presence could be different and that's why she couldn't hold on.

Yes, we get used to Jesus, how we view him, and how we understand him, the way he speaks to us and the encouragement he gives us.

But Jesus speaks to us as well when he says, *"Do not hold on to me;"* he says, "Don't you remember I ascended to the Father? Don't you remember you know me through the work of the Holy Spirit? Haven't you read what I said about how the wind blows where it chooses, and you hear the sound of it, but you do not know where it comes from or where it goes?"

Don't try to hold on to the last gust of wind; don't try to hold on to the way God chose to come among his people in first century Palestine assuming it will always be like that. Remember that he still comes, he still surprises us, and he still turns people's lives upside down – maybe even still up to three or four times in a few days. Because of Jesus, but in very different ways, it is still true that hope dawns, love triumphs and life has the last word.

Look at the world around us and notice just a few things: *"God shows no partiality."*[31] No-one is outside God's care. Those who have been forgotten and marginalised by society have been brought into focus by the creation of food banks, many by churches, which allows us to quantify the level of hunger in Britain and put it on the nation's agenda.

Those who have been driven from their homes and countries by oppression, violence and persecution and forced to flee in fear, risking everything to cross land and sea to places of safety and dehumanised by authorities overwhelmed by their plight have been brought into focus by the human pictures and the demand for a humane response and the offer of hospitality – much of it by churches.

In a Thought for the Day[32] Lord Singh pointed out that in celebrating Baisakhi, Sikhs were *"marking a commitment to human rights first made in 1699 and putting ethical imperatives before political or social expediency … recognising the oneness of our human family, with a total rejection of all notions of caste or race"*.

What have you seen that shows the dawning of hope, the triumph of love and life having the last word?

Whatever you've seen, Jesus says, "Don't hold on to me, to the old ways, to what you know, but go and tell…"

---

[31] Acts 10:34 (NIV)
[32] BBC Radio 4, 14 April 2014

Sermon Note to Preachers and Listeners

Interaction

The first sermon on Fruit Trees[33] illustrates an interactive opening to a sermon. Not easy to get a sense of in written form but it can be an engaging way to begin. Questions and answers engage people so that they feel part of the event. Just joining in by answering some questions at the beginning engages people's interest and helps them to feel like participants rather than simply listeners.

One minister I worked with sometimes used to do a competitive comprehension exercise on the passage with one side of the church against the other. They'd have to put their copies of the reading away and answer questions about it with bonuses offered to the other side after a wrong answer. This was fun in an 'All Age' setting and had the merit of enabling an engagement with the passage but the sense of competition was not necessarily affirming to people with memory problems or those who struggled at school.

The advantages of the kind of quiz in the Fruit Trees sermon are that it is quick, on message and there are no points involved – and therefore no prizes either. The quiz illustrated in this sermon gets people thinking about what sort of fruit grows on what sort of plants. It starts deliberately very easy so anyone could answer. ("What fruit grows on apple trees?" "And plum trees?") This builds a rapport with any congregation, even one where the preacher has not preached before. The third question ("What fruit grows on a vine?") deliberately requires just a little more thought and builds the expectation of a sermon that is in some way horticultural. The mood is then deliberately lightened by reference to the nursery rhyme. When asked, "What grows on a little nut tree?" most congregations will answer, "Nuts."

---

[33] See p.29

This kind of quiz can easily be done very quickly. If the facilities and the preparation time are available, it can be jazzed up a little by using pictures and adding captions for the answers and a picture illustrating the nursery rhyme at the end.

This kind of quiz or question-and-answer session for an introduction can be tailored to almost any sermon as a way in. It is an engaging opening, involving the congregation and enabling participation. It is more interesting than simply stating or asserting something that is true or a paraphrase of something from the reading. It is likely that it means the preacher keeps the listeners' interest for longer.

If the facilities are available to show pictures, this kind of quiz can also be done as an odd-one-out quiz, about four pictures on a similar theme, one of which is in some way different. If a number could be odd-ones-out for different reasons, preacher and congregation can have a laugh together about that as long as the intended reason is stressed and has something to do with the theme. An example might be a way into the sermon on soils from the Parable of the Sower. Pictures of a path, a rocky outcrop, a wildflower meadow and an arable farmer's field, each with some weeds or wild flowers growing except in the field, would be an obvious odd-one-out quiz; the odd-one-out being the field because it's the only one producing wheat ready for harvest.

The current trend towards just about every TV programme seeking responses from viewers may be annoying to some but it does seem to get engagement and thought about the programme's subject. A quiz or question-and-answer session at the beginning of a sermon enables engagement and involvement from the beginning and probably prompts more thought about the subject matter as the preacher goes on.

The 'Yes, but How?' Moment

Many sermons have what I call a 'yes, but how?' moment. The one in this collection on John 15 makes this explicit but many are implicit. Some go unnoticed by preacher and congregation but it is likely that someone listening will spot it.

The 'yes, but how?' moment is the point in the sermon where you've taken the congregation with you through the theological meat of the message, you've made a good point and made it well. Possibly everyone is awed by your analysis of the passage and your spiritual insight. They may even have bought into a controversial statement of what ought to be the case in relationships within the church or what God requires of his people.

If you find endings difficult, this is usually one point at which to stop. Everyone will say it was a good point well made and commend you for your analysis and insight. But they will go away slightly dissatisfied unless they are specifically looking only for something intellectually stimulating. The problem with ending at that point is that it is the 'yes, but how?' moment.

Ask yourself, what is the desired effect of this sermon; what do I want this sermon to do? Your answer will probably be that you want hearers to do something; to change in some way as a result of hearing it; to go about their spiritual lives differently, to become involved in something or take part in something with renewed enthusiasm, seeing it from a new faith perspective.

With the sermon on John 15 and Jesus' saying, *I am the true vine,* I pointed out the 'yes, but how?' moment. This is where I hope I had taken hearers (or readers) through some fairly complex theology about 'remaining in him' – being connected to the vine. Probably most people would have been nodding wisely saying to themselves, "Yes, I need to remain in Christ, that's an important point to be reminded of from this passage." That's the 'yes' bit.

If I'd stopped there they might even have gone away with a very positive feel about the sermon. But if they got home and had roast preacher for lunch they'd have thought a little bit longer and realised they'd inwardly committed themselves to remaining in Christ but now they were on their own. Up to that point they had been given no idea how to do that. What followed was the application; how, in practical terms, they could go about ensuring that they knew they were branches connected with the vine.

So, as you listen to sermons, read sermons or prepare sermons, watch out for the 'yes, but how?' moment.

The 'What's That All About Then?' Moment

The sermon on the wheat and the weeds takes much longer than many of the others in this collection to identify the actual point of Jesus' teaching. About half the sermon extends the gardening or agricultural ideas, pointing out cultural similarities and differences in order to gain as much understanding of the gardening side of the parable as possible. By about half way it has explored the question all the way round and intensified something that was probably around for Jesus' original hearers.

Many times when he taught, including the end of the explanation of the Parable of the Weeds, Jesus ended with the phrase, *"Whoever has ears, let them hear."* It could be paraphrased as, "If you've really been listening you can work that one out for yourself."

By working up the same question in listeners' minds and then posing that question half way through, this sermon takes people who are situated in a very different context to the same question as original listeners may have had. It is possible that Jesus explained this parable because it raised questions, so the sermon also raises a question. Often when we read Jesus' teaching it is tempting to wonder, "So what's that all about then?" as his hearers may also have done. Sometimes, even when he gives an explanation, we still have the same question going around in our heads.

It is helpful for preachers and listeners alike to watch for (and even deliberately include) a 'what's that all about then?' moment. Spinning listeners along with an extended 'slantwise' introduction can get people intrigued, asking a similar question and wide open to the main point when it comes in very simple and direct form.

'What's that all about then?' is a question applied to either the passage or the sermon, or both. In the sermon on the wheat and the weeds it can be asked of both. Listeners should watch for a 'what's that all about then?' moment in a sermon when they're wondering where a slantwise introduction is leading. This poses the question of the sermon's real subject for listeners. It is a helpful device to include as a preacher, raising the interest levels and provoking questions. If provoking the question in relation to the sermon can be combined with raising the question in relation to the biblical text, especially in the way original hearers or readers may have been questioning, it is at least 'buy one get one free'.

Sermon listeners can be more engaged with the preaching if they're looking for a 'what's that all about then?' moment and have that question in mind as the readings are read and as the preacher begins. If listeners go away with aspects of the question still going around in their heads, it does not mean the preacher has failed. It may be that the preacher has simply done as Jesus did. I'm sure many people went away from his teaching wondering, "So what's that all about then?" – especially when he ended, "Whoever has ears, let them hear."

The 'Time for You to Talk' Moment

What I'm calling the 'time for you to talk' sermon could come in two different forms: the 'time for you to talk after the service' type and the 'time for you to talk during the sermon' type. The latter I'll come to in a moment and is not easy to illustrate in written form. The former could be illustrated by most of the sermons in this book.

In two churches where I minister we have a monthly opportunity for half an hour after the service when we've all had a cup of coffee to ask questions and discuss issues raised by the sermon. We call it 'Time to Talk' and I usually start by reminding them that I've been talking and now it's time for them to talk. This requires preaching in a way that Tom Long describes as "like I want them to talk".[34]

It is also said that there are often at least as many sermons heard as there are people in the room. A 'Time to Talk' session after the service gives people an opportunity to air the one they heard. It can be interesting for preachers to discover what incidental points have been taken away by listeners and which key theological themes have hardly registered. It is also helpful to listeners to check whether others heard something similar or indeed whether the preacher actually said something that they found interesting, helpful, challenging or particularly odd.

More importantly, it gives people an opportunity to answer three questions which it is good to have in mind whenever we listen to any talk, lecture or sermon:

- What was the best thing the speaker said? Or what did I most agree with?
- What was the worst thing the speaker said? Or what did I most disagree with?
- And what was the best thing the speaker didn't say? Or what was the brilliant point that I would have made but the speaker didn't?

'Time for you to talk' sermons in this sense are likely to be ones that either address aspects of a contemporary issue or include or end with the 'what's that all about then?' moment that we looked at in the previous sermon note. A 'time for you to talk' sermon opens up

---

[34] College of Preachers event, London 2011

questions and prompts debate and question rather than closes down an issue by providing all the answers.

The other sort of 'time for you to talk' sermon can't be illustrated in written form because it will take its direction from the responses from the congregation. We live in a questioning age that doesn't defer to authorities on any subject but takes self-selected contributors' comments on issues with as much validity as those of professors and those who've researched and written books. There may be space and technology available in your church for such dialogue within the sermon during the service. It doesn't have to be computers, specially selected mobile numbers, email addresses or Facebook and Twitter accounts; a roving microphone would do.

Where possible, this kind of 'sermon' could be encouraged from time to time. It might be a good interactive, open and helpful way of engaging with people at occasions where a large proportion present are unfamiliar with church. Café services, where the emphasis is on café rather than service, may lend themselves to this. In a culture where people are more familiar with the phone-in format or sending in comments to their radio and TV programmes by text, email, Facebook or Twitter it could be appropriate to have 'time for you to talk' sermons of this type.

These would briefly open up an issue from a biblical and Christian perspective and invite comments and questions from those present who have experience or connections with the subject. It would probably need careful coordinating and facilitation by someone other than the 'preacher' who would be the equivalent of the studio expert filling in the results of research or traditional or orthodox Christian belief.

This kind of event invites engagement and participation. 'Preachers' at such events need the courage not to try to persuade or come across as telling people what they ought to believe. Listeners need to be willing and able to assess contributions from all comers and go away without answers but plenty on which to ponder.

'What Happened?' or 'What's Going On?'

It is almost inescapable when preaching that we repeat or retell part or all of the biblical narrative from the text. I have heard many times of preachers who seem only to do that. It means that listeners go home knowing what happened. When the passage is reiterated we get to know and remember the biblical accounts – we know our Bible better. That is a good thing. But it is not enough.

There is another aspect to preaching which flows from the 'what's that all about then?' question.[35] We may often ask that about a text and sometimes of a sermon; being left with a question to go away and puzzle out as those 'with ears to hear' is a good thing. But listeners are entitled to more than a retelling of a biblical narrative; they should be given more than an account of what happened.

This is where I draw the distinction between what happened and what's going on.

What happened is the retelling, perhaps in our own words, of the biblical passage. What's going on attempts to unfold something of the meaning for listeners and readers past and present.

Unpacking what's going on will include some or all of a number of factors:

- Explaining some of the word play that has been hidden by translation.
- Pointing out connections that are obscured by distance of time, geography or culture.
- Pointing out connections with other biblical ideas and events.
- Pointing out connections with other ideas and events familiar to listeners; ideas that are contemporary, historical or literary.
- Spelling out and explaining the theological ideas behind or illustrated by the events described in the text.

All of this helps with listeners' understanding of what's going on as distinct from simply improving their knowledge of what happened.

---

[35] See page 109

What Shall I Read Next?

Publisher's Recommendation

The Song in the Gate

Alan Hoare

ISBN 978-1-910197-68-4 / 978-1-910197-69-1

This inspiring daily devotional takes the reader through Psalm 1, over 24 days, with in depth revelation and practical application.

"Here is where we cut our teeth in praying, as we take upon our lips the prayers of others. As we make our way through the psalms – praying, singing, weeping – we will become more and more aware of the God who inspired them in the first place. They will bring us to both an intimacy with, and a deep, holy respect for, the Father, the Son and the Holy Spirit."

"I commend the reading of this devotional pilgrimage."
Chris Bowater, International Worship Ministry

"I'm convinced that all who read it will be encouraged, spiritually fed and, most important of all, be brought closer to the God we love and serve. Read, mark, learn and inwardly digest!"
Ishmael, Singer / Songwriter,

"...bite-sized nuggets of easy-to-understand yet challenging and life-changing theology. Great stuff!"
Andy Piercy, Singer / Songwriter